Mediterranean Diet for Beginners

The Complete Guide with 60 Delicious Recipes and

a

7-Day Meal Plan to Lose Weight the Healthy Way

PUBLISHED BY: Mark Evans

Copyright © 2019 All rights reserved.

No part of this publication may be copied, reproduced in any format, by any means, electronic or otherwise, without prior consent from the copyright owner and publisher of this book.

Table of Contents

Introduction 4
Chapter 1: The Mediterranean Diet............................... 6
Chapter 2: Eating the Mediterranean Diet..................... 9
Chapter 3: The Health Benefits of the Mediterranean Diet..16
Chapter 4: The Mediterranean Lifestyle 21
Chapter 5: Shopping Mediterranean............................... 25
Chapter 6: Cooking Tips and Techniques 31
Chapter 7: Ideas to Incorporate More Plant-Based Foods Into Your Diet 33
Chapter 8: Tips for the Beginners 35
Chapter 9: Meal Planning.. 37
Chapter 10: Breakfast Recipes 40
Chapter 11: Lunch Recipes.. 55
Chapter 12: Dinner Recipes 72
Chapter 13: Appetizers and Snacks 91
Chapter 14: Salad and Soup Recipes 106
Chapter 15: Pasta and Couscous..................................... 122
Chapter 16: Dessert Recipes 140
Conclusion 158
Thank you 159

Introduction

If you are looking for an effective way of losing excess weight, achieve better health and longevity, then this Mediterranean diet book is for you. This book is all about the Mediterranean diet and lifestyle. This book is a comprehensive and easy-to-follow guide for beginners and advanced users. The Mediterranean diet is a different form of diet that is both easy to follow and meant to be a lifestyle change. Whether you are looking to improve your heart health, lose weight, or achieve longevity, the Mediterranean diet can help you with that.

Enjoy all of the amazing benefits of the Mediterranean diet, no matter how busy your schedule. This Mediterranean diet cookbook is your ultimate guide. By following it, you will know the essentials about the Mediterranean diet. You will learn how to live as the Mediterranean do, you will learn how to eat, drink, and truly enjoy life while becoming the healthiest version of you.

This book takes a simplified approach to cooking. The wide variety of recipes might surprise you, and you will not feel deprived or hungry any more. The recipes are bursting with flavor, easy to prepare, and sure to please everyone at your table. Experienced and novice cooks alike will be inspired by these recipes and cooking the Mediterranean way will be a breeze even on your weeknights. So flip over to the next page now and have a happy and successful Mediterranean diet living!

Chapter 1: The Mediterranean Diet

The Mediterranean diet consists of plates full of colorful, healthy, and wholesome food. The Mediterranean diet revolves around healthier, sustainable principles of eating and living. The Mediterranean diet is more than just a diet; it is a lifestyle that has been created over centuries of healthy living and bonding for food. Families from all around the Mediterranean coast have contributed for years to what we know today as the Mediterranean diet. The Mediterranean diet consisting of eating whole, unprocessed foods, such as whole grains, vegetables, fruits, fresh seafood, good fats from nuts, seeds, and olive oil.

These are the staple foods of a Mediterranean diet, though good-quality poultry, meat, dairy, and red wine make appearances as well. The diet is rich in antioxidants, vitamins, and omega- 3 oil due to the variety of fish, fresh fruit, and vegetables incorporated into the diet. Ultimately, the Mediterranean diet is not a diet and a lifestyle that includes healthy eating, daily physical exercise, and daily healthy social interactions with friends and family. It is a lifestyle that keeps you in better shape, improves longevity, and helps you to achieve emotional well-being.

The foods that we eat have been known to contribute greatly to how our health turns out. Feeding on unhealthy foods is known to cause a variety of health issues, including high blood pressure, high cholesterol, heart disease, diabetes, and even cancer. The Mediterranean diet is considered as one of the world's healthiest diet. As the diet is considered more of a lifestyle, it should be adopted as a daily practice and a way of living that is sustainable. The Mediterranean diet incorporates traditional and healthy living habits of people from the countries that border the Mediterranean Sea, such as Spain, France, Italy, Greece, Morocco and the like. The diet varies by country and the region it is adopted, so it may have a range of definitions.

History

The Mediterranean diet originates from the area known as "the Mediterranean basin". Historians call it "the cradle of civilization." The Mediterranean basin includes countries such as Spain, Italy, France, Greece, Turkey, Morocco, and many other countries and islands.
The origins of "Mediterranean Diet" got lost in history, although we know it takes its influence from three different parts of Europe. The first is the Romans, whose meals consisted of bread, olive oil, and wine. Besides these, the rich feasted on fresh seafood. Germanic countries are the second

influence. They lived in green lands and forest full of fruits and berries. They grew vegetables and raise animals. Christian missionaries bonded both cultures. Lastly, Arabic countries contributed to the spices. Mediterranean food is issued from these three major countries from the past.

In 1958, American scientist Ancel Keys conducted a study, known as "the Seven Countries Study" to find a correlation between cholesterol and heart disease. The study includes Japan, United States, Finland, Italy, the Netherlands, Greece, and the former Yugoslavia. The research revealed that the healthiest people were those who ate a diet consisting mainly of vegetables, grains, fruits, beans, and fish. The residents of the Mediterranean island of Crete, Greece were in the best shape. The researchers concluded that it is the diet that keeps them in the best shape; hence the concept of the "Mediterranean Diet."

However, the diet only became popular when Harvard University's School of Public Health published "Eat, Drink and Be Healthy: The Harvard Medical School Guide to Healthy Eating." in 1993. In 2010, the United Nations Educational, Scientific, and Cultural Organization, (UNESCO) recognized the Mediterranean Diet as a fundamental part of the history.

Chapter 2: Eating the Mediterranean Diet

The main components of the Mediterranean diet:

1. Whole grains: Whole grains are rich with fiber, vitamins, and phytochemicals, and are an integral part of the Mediterranean diet. Research has shown that whole grains can lower the risk of diabetes, heart disease, and cancer. A whole grain kernel consists of an outer layer, the bran (fiber); a middle layer (protein and complex carbohydrates); and an inner layer (protein, vitamins, and minerals). Examples of whole grains that are common to the Mediterranean diet are quinoa, oatmeal, kasha, and barley. Consume 3 to 5 servings of whole grains daily.
2. Fresh fruits and vegetables: Fruits and vegetables contain an abundance of fiber, vitamins, minerals, and complex carbohydrates that lower the risk of heart disease and cancer. Phytonutrients – a powerful plant-derived nutrient (concentrated in the skin of fruits and vegetables) helps fight disease and improve our health. It is recommended that we eat a wide

variety of colors (spinach, yellow squash, red apples, blueberries, oranges, etc.) in order to get all the nutritional benefits that fruits and vegetables can provide. You need to eat at least 4 servings of fresh fruits and vegetables per day.

3. Fish: Oily fish is another component of the Mediterranean diet. They are a rich source of protein and omega-3 fatty acids. Omega-3 fatty acids help lower triglyceride and cholesterol levels and lower the risk of heart attack. They also reduce inflammation. The best choices are flounder, Pollock, trout, shad, sardines, herring, tuna, albacore, and salmon. Avoid king mackerel, shark, swordfish, and tilefish as these fish species tend to have the highest mercury content. Eat at least 3 servings per week.

4. Nuts: Nuts like almonds and walnuts are rich in omega-3 and monounsaturated fat, as well as good sources of fiber, protein, and vitamins. Several clinical trials have demonstrated that regular nut consumption lowers cholesterol, lowers risk of heart disease and heart attack.

5. Beans (legumes): Beans are a rich source of soluble and insoluble fiber and help subdue appetite and lower cholesterol. Also, beans are a good source of protein and vitamins. Regular bean consumption lowers the risk of diabetes, heart disease, and cancer.

6. Olive oil: Olive oil is the "soul" of the Mediterranean diet. Rich in monounsaturated fat, olive oil is beneficial for heart health. The regular use of olive oil is associated with a reduced risk of inflammatory disorders, heart disease, diabetes, and cancer. Olive oil also lowers bad cholesterol levels and increase good cholesterol levels, and makes our bodies less susceptible to oxidative damage by free radicals. Additionally, olive oil can help you lose weight.
7. Healthful fats: Healthful fats are an essential part of the Mediterranean diet. Get them from olives, olive oil, avocados, nuts, seeds, fresh fish, and shellfish.
8. Dairy products: Consume milk, cheese, and yogurt in moderation. Choose low-fat milk, cheeses, and eat Greek yogurt. Consume up to 7 servings of dairy products per week.
9. Eggs: Opt for free-range, organic, hormone-free eggs. They contain more omega-3 fats than commercial eggs. Enjoy 3 to 5 servings (2 eggs) of eggs per week.
10. Poultry: Poultry is preferred in the Mediterranean diet than red meat. Eat chicken and turkey. Also, include game birds such as pigeon, pheasant, duck, and quail. Eat 2 to 5 servings per week.
11. Red meat: Red meats such as lamb, beef, and pork are usually reserved for a few special meals. Choose organic, grass-fed meats because they are higher in

omega-3s. You can eat 3 to 5 servings of red meat per month.

12. Sweets: The Mediterranean dessert usually includes cheese and/or fruit, not sugar-rich cakes and pastries. Artificial sweeteners are not recommended. Stick with honey, sugar, and molasses in small quantities. You can consume up to 4 servings of sweets per week.

13. Red wine: Red wine is better than other forms of alcohol. Red wine contains resveratrol and polyphenols. Both of these improve your heart health and lower your risk of heart disease. Resveratrol has a beneficial impact on blood clotting, lowers bad cholesterol levels and increases good cholesterol levels. You need to consume red wine in moderation (only a couple of 5-ounce glasses daily). Grape juice is an alternative to red wine. Purple grape juice lowers the risk of heart attack.

14. Salt: The Mediterranean diet is low in sodium. Limit using salt and focus on fresh herbs and spices to flavor your food.

What to eat and avoid at a glance

The basics:
- Eat: Fish, seafood, whole grains, breads, potatoes, legumes, seeds, nuts, fruits, vegetables, extra virgin olive oil, herbs, and spices.
- In moderation: Yogurt, cheese, eggs, and poultry
- Rarely: Red meat
- Don't eat: Refined oils, refined grains, processed meat, highly processed foods, added sugars, and sugar-sweetened beverages.

Avoid these unhealthy foods:
- Highly processed foods: Anything labeled as "diet" or "low-fat"
- Processed meat: Hot dogs, processed sausages, etc.
- Refined oils: cottonseed oil, canola oil, soybean oil, and others
- Trans fats: Avoid them completely (such as margarine).
- Refined grains: Products made from refined grains
- Added sugar: Table sugar, ice cream, candies, soda, and others.

Foods to eat:
- Vegetables: Cucumbers, Brussels sprouts, carrots, cauliflower, spinach, etc.
- Fruits: Melons, figs, grapes, pears, oranges, bananas, etc.
- Nuts and seeds: All types of nuts and seeds.
- Legumes: Peanuts, chickpeas, pulses, lentils, peas, beans, etc.
- Tubers: Turnips, yams, potatoes, sweet potatoes, etc.
- Whole grains: Whole grain bread, pasta, whole wheat, buckwheat, corn, barley, rye, brown rice, whole oats.
- Fish and seafood: Shrimp, mackerel, tuna, trout, sardines, salmon, clams, crab, mussels, etc.
- Poultry: Duck, turkey, chicken, etc.
- Dairy: Greek yogurt, cheese, etc.
- Healthy fats: olives, extra virgin olive oil, avocados, and avocado oil

What to drink:
- You can drink about 1 glass of red wine per day.
- Tea and coffee are also acceptable.
- Avoid sugar-sweetened fruit juices and beverages.

How to follow the diet when eating out?
- Only eat whole-grain bread. Avoid butter and opt for olive oil.

- Choose fish or seafood as your main dish.
- Ask them to use olive oil to cook your food.

Chapter 3: The Health Benefits of the Mediterranean Diet

The Mediterranean diet is a tasty way to eat and it is also a sustainable way to lower inflammation. It is the inflammation that triggers most of the modern diseases, including cardiovascular disease, diabetes, and cancer. The U.S. News ranked the Mediterranean diet as the best overall diet in 2019 (https://health.usnews.com/best-diet).

The Mediterranean diet includes plenty of fresh, non-starchy foods. Here are some of the benefits of the Mediterranean diet:

1. A healthy way to lose weight: If you are looking for a diet that will help you lose weight, then the Mediterranean diet is the best approach. Many people around the world follow this diet to lose weight. Fiber-rich Mediterranean food items ensure fullness. Fiber-rich foods make you feel full quickly. The fiber also helps with increased metabolism and healthy weight loss. The key is avoiding simple carbs with fibrous vegetables, fruits, beans, and legumes. The diet can help you eat low-carb and high-protein foods if you

wish. Plenty of quality dairy products and high amount of seafood make sure there is no feeling of deprivation.
    - https://www.nejm.org/doi/full/10.1056/NEJMoa0708681
2. Improves heart health: Research shows that healthy omega-3 and monounsaturated fat-rich Mediterranean diet lowers dieters' risk of heart disease. The study shows that olive oil can decrease the risk of sudden cardiac death by 45% and the risk of cardiac death by 30%. Other studies show that consuming olive oil lowers high blood pressure when compared with vegetable oil.
    - https://www.ncbi.nlm.nih.gov/pubmed/17058434
    - https://www.ncbi.nlm.nih.gov/pubmed/23939686
3. Helps fight cancer: A diet that includes lots of fruits and vegetables can protect DNA from damage, prevent cell mutation, lower inflammation, fight cancer and delay tumor growth. The study shows that following the Mediterranean diet that includes a balanced ratio of omega-3 and omega-6 fatty acids, a high amount of antioxidants, fiber and polyphenols (found in vegetables, fruit, olive oil, and wine) lower risk of cancer.

- https://www.ncbi.nlm.nih.gov/pubmed/22644232
4. Benefits post-menopausal women: It is known that menopause can lower women's bone and muscle mass. On the other hand, eating the Mediterranean diet can have a positive impact on bone and muscle mass loss.
    - https://www.sciencedaily.com/releases/2018/03/180318144826.htm
5. Prevents and treats diabetes: The Mediterranean diet is an anti-inflammatory diet, which means it can lower diseases that are caused by inflammation such as type 2 diabetes and metabolic syndrome. The diet controls excess insulin production. It is the excess insulin that triggers weight gain and makes us obese.
    - https://www.ncbi.nlm.nih.gov/pubmed/19689829
6. Protects cognitive health and can improve your mood: Healthy fats of the Mediterranean diet is good for your brain. The Mediterranean diets act as a natural Alzheimer's and Parkinson's disease treatment. Anti-inflammatory veggies, fruits, and healthy fats like olive oil and nuts are known to fight age-related cognitive decline. This helps counter the harmful effects of free radicals and toxicity which degrade brain function. The first and second studies (below)

show that dieters who follow the Mediterranean diet were less likely to develop Alzheimer's disease. The third study shows that there is a link between eating more fish and reduced risk of Alzheimer's. Probiotic foods like kefir and yogurt can improve mood disorders and cognitive function.

- https://www.ncbi.nlm.nih.gov/pmc/articles/PMC5538737/
- https://www.ncbi.nlm.nih.gov/pubmed/16622828
- https://www.ncbi.nlm.nih.gov/pubmed/19262590

7. Strengthens bones: Consuming olive oil helps preserve bone density by increasing the maturation and proliferation of bone cells. Another study reveals that the Mediterranean diet can help prevent osteoporosis.

- https://www.ncbi.nlm.nih.gov/pubmed/24975408
- https://www.ncbi.nlm.nih.gov/pubmed/22946650

8. Good for your gut: Study shows that Mediterranean diet followers had a higher percentage of good bacteria in their gut. Scientists concluded that eating more plant-based foods such as fruits, vegetables, and legumes boost good bacteria production up to 7%.

- https://www.frontiersin.org/articles/10.3389/fnut.2018.00028/full
9. Fights depression and lowers anxiety: Doctors recommend the Mediterranean diet as a treatment for patients with anxiety, depression, and other mental health issues. Food items like egg, spinach, and kale contain carotenoids. This substance boosts the good bacteria in your gut and your mood. Recent studies show that eating the Mediterranean diet can help lower the risk of depression.
    - https://www.practiceupdate.com/content/healthy-dietary-choices-may-reduce-the-risk-of-depression/74278
    - https://www.ncbi.nlm.nih.gov/pubmed/29775747
10. Helps you live longer: Eating a diet based on fresh and unprocessed produce and healthy fats can help you live longer. Studies show that monounsaturated fat is linked with lower levels of inflammatory disease such as depression, heart disease, cancer, cognitive decline, and Alzheimer's disease.
    - https://www.ahajournals.org/doi/pdf/10.1161/01.cir.99.6.779

Chapter 4: The Mediterranean Lifestyle

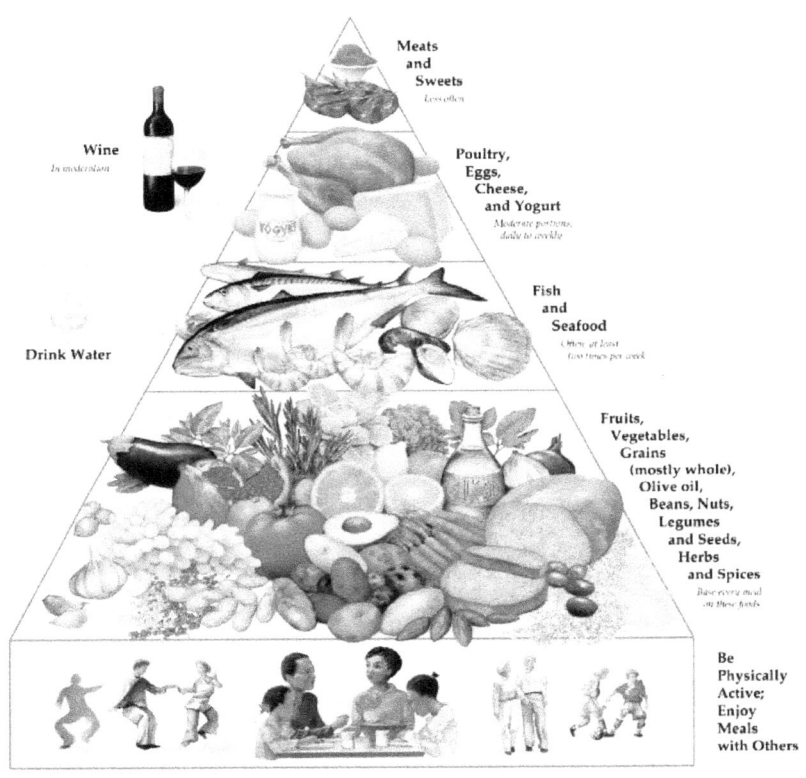

Some people find it surprising that the base of the Mediterranean Diet Pyramid is not a food group, but behaviors such as social interaction and physical activity. At its core, the Mediterranean diet is not a diet in the orthodox sense of the world. It is a lifestyle that should be enjoyed with both health and pleasure in mind.

Physical activity

The Mediterranean's philosophy of approaching life with an equal measure of health and pleasure leads to a more balanced and happy living. For most people, physical activity means going to the gym after work after sitting an entire day in their cars, at their desks, or on their couches.

The concept of physical activity is different in the Mediterranean region. Daily life in the Mediterranean region requires more natural activity and calorie expenditure. The Mediterranean lifestyle encourages people to walk when going to places instead of using cars and public transports. Driving and parking are discouraged, and facilities are provided so people walk more when going to places. Simple tasks such as shopping, cooking, drying, and ironing require greater effort and expenditure of calories. To achieve optimal benefit from the Mediterranean diet, dieters need to integrate pleasurable forms of activity into their daily lives.

Camaraderie & Companionship

Family life is valued greatly in the Mediterranean region. Every culture and country around the Mediterranean encourages people to eat together. Eating alone in the region is strictly prohibited. Only people who live alone can eat by themselves. Although times have changed, most people in the Mediterranean consider it unpleasant to eat alone. This is why school and work schedules revolve around mealtimes. Families try to eat at least one meal together daily, even if they have a hectic work schedule.

Recent data shows that residents of Sardina (an island in the Mediterranean) are ten times more likely to reach a hundred years old, than Americans. Researchers reveal that the key to longevity is the family style of eating. Scientists concluded that there is something deeply satisfying about enjoying meals as a family, which promotes longevity. Family mealtimes trigger a deep sense of psychological comfort and security, which has a positive effect on health and happiness.

Food is viewed as a way to express thanks, love, appreciation, and respect in the Mediterranean region. In European countries of the Mediterranean region, such as France, Greece, Italy, and Spain, great pride is taken in giving a loved one or guest a home-cooked food item. The gift is especially significant if the food is grown in the presenter's own land.

Ground rules for family mealtimes:
- Completely avoid electronics and TV.
- Discuss only good news and pleasant topics.
- No unpleasant or off-limit topics.

- Set an attractive table.
- Dress for the meal.

In today's busy life, it might be considered as a Utopian fantasy, but here are a few tips on implementing the Mediterranean lifestyle:

- Treat your food, friends, and family as an integral part of life.
- If you are not doing it already, then socialize with family, friends, and co-workers during mealtimes.
- Make easy make-ahead meals to work into your schedule.
- Include a variety of food items into your diet.
- Find enjoyable ways to incorporate exercise in your life, such as walking with a friend or gardening.
- Vow to live each day with both peace and health in mind.

Chapter 5: Shopping Mediterranean

Living the Mediterranean lifestyle involves making a few changes in your grocery shopping. The first step to restocking your kitchen is finding the best stores and markets to meet your needs, which involves planning.

Knowing where to shop
Most Americans shop from the nearest grocery store, and on the Mediterranean diet, the grocery store is still the best place to find your staples. No matter where you live, shopping local is the best idea. Many people in the Mediterranean depend on the produce stands, local markets, butchers, and bakers to get the freshest produce. Big grocery stores are convenient, but usually, they import food items from different states or countries. The longer the transport time, the more nutrients are lost. So ideally, you should shop from the local farmer's market. Local farmers' markets are a wonderful resource to get fresh, seasonal food for any community. Besides getting fresh fruits, the other benefits of buying from the farmers' market include the following:

1. The food items are local, so they are fresh, seasonal, and more nutrient-rich.
2. The local market gives you an opportunity to walk to your store, which is a part of the Mediterranean lifestyle.

3. Buying local is a great way to give back to your community.
4. Shopping locally gives you a similar Mediterranean experience.

Here is a link to find a local farmers' market in your area (https://www.localharvest.org/)

Local CSA

Buying a share of a Community Supported Agriculture (CSA) is a great way to incorporate fresh, seasonal produce into your diet. You pay an upfront fee to a local farm and receive a box of fresh produce every week. Going with a CSA gives you the feeling of growing your own produce. This is also a great way to get into the Mediterranean style of living. However, CSA isn't for everyone. If you don't enjoy a wide variety, and you're picky with produce, then you may not enjoy CSA.

- https://www.ifoam.bio/en/community-supported-agriculture-csa

Other good spots
There are other uncommon places to find foods that work well with a Mediterranean lifestyle. Here are some hot spots for Mediterranean shopping:
- Mediterranean markets

- Bakeries
- Butchers
- Greek markets
- Italian markets
- Greek or Italian restaurants that also sell groceries

Finding the right products

Buying produce

Buying for the Mediterranean diet includes three main criteria: local proximity, seasonality, and freshness. When shopping for produce, you need to:

- Avoid bruises and wilting: They are signs that the produce has passed its peak.
- Avoid products that are too ripe. Pick produce that is just ripe enough.
- Go for variety: Choose a variety of produce.

Seafood

- Avoid fish with dulling or darkening color around the edges.
- The skin should be metallic and shiny.
- The grill should be tight against the body.
- The flesh should be firm and elastic.
- Avoid fish that has a strong odor.

Beef, pork, and poultry
- Pork chops should be firm.
- Poultry should not have a strong odor and look firm.
- Beef should have a solid color.

Dairy
- The grocery's deli cold case or refrigerated section offers a variety of dairy products.
- You can always shop online.

Grains and breads
- You will find the rice products in the inner aisles of your grocery store.
- Buy bread made with whole grains, instead of white flour.
- Sourdough bread is another option.

Loading up your pantry

Here is a must-have pantry list:
- Bread
- Oatmeal
- Pasta
- Quinoa, pearl barley, or bulgur wheat
- Rice (both brown and wild rice)

- Canned soups, such as tomato, vegetables, and minestrone
- Lentils
- Canned and/or dried beans
- Seasonings and herbs, including rosemary, thyme, oregano, basil, tarragon, parsley, dill, cinnamon, ginger, curry powder, chili powder, garlic powder, paprika, ground cumin, black pepper, sea salt, and salt.
- Oils, including canola oil, olive oil, extra-virgin olive oil.
- Unsweetened cocoa
- Sugars, including light or dark brown sugar, and granulated sugar
- Flours, including all-purpose, oat, wheat-bran, whole-wheat
- Extracts, such as almond, anise, and pure vanilla
- Cornmeal
- Dry yeast
- Baking powder, cornstarch, baking soda

Refrigerator items
- Condiments, such as mayonnaise, salsas, Worcestershire sauce, and mustard
- Natural nut butter like almond butter and peanut butter

- Nuts
- Milk or cottage cheese
- Cheese
- Plain Greek yogurt
- Fresh vegetables
- Carton of eggs

Freezer items

- Precooked recipes such as chilis, stews, soups
- Ground beef
- Frozen shrimp
- Fish fillets
- Chicken breasts
- Frozen fruits
- Frozen vegetables
- Frozen spinach

Countertop items

- Avocados
- Onions and garlic
- Tomatoes
- Lemons
- Fruits for the fruit bowl (such as pears, bananas, oranges, apples)

Chapter 6: Cooking Tips and Techniques

Preparing foods at home instead of eating out or relying on restaurants and convenience foods is part of the Mediterranean lifestyle.

Scheduling time for cooking

Home cooking is an integral part of the Mediterranean lifestyle. It encourages you to eat fresh, plant-based foods and lowers your dependency on prepackaged meals. Here are a few ideas to incorporate cooking into your schedule:

- o   If you are really busy, then use your off days and weekends cooking meals in batches and freezing them. This will make following the Mediterranean diet easier.
- o   If you have very little time for cooking, then choose recipes that take less time.
- o   Rearrange your schedule to find time to cook dinner several nights a week.
- o   As a beginner, keep your cooking process simple. Start with dishes that take little prep time and no

precooking. When you get used to Mediterranean cooking, choose more complex dishes.

Batch cooking
- o Cook several dishes such as casseroles, lasagnas, chilies, stews, and soups during your weekend. Freeze them in the freezer and eat during busy weekdays.
- o Prepare some foods: You can precook whole grains, sauces, and beans. Use them in various dishes.
- o Make more freezer-friendly meals: For example, you can cook a large batch of grilled chicken, freeze them and use them with steamed veggies, sandwiches, burritos, and salads.

Finding high-quality olive oil
- o Generally, high quality extra-virgin olive oil is stored in dark glass containers.
- o Choose a grassy, spicy flavor because they are the best quality.
- o Check out the harvest date.

Chapter 7: Ideas to Incorporate More Plant-Based Foods Into Your Diet

Here are a few more tips on the Mediterranean diet:

1. Eat a variety of vegetables as a snack. Pre-slice different vegetables, such as carrots, broccoli, bell peppers and others for the whole week. You can eat them with dips.
2. Eat more fruit or vegetable with your every meal. For example, you can eat some fruit with yogurt, include tomatoes, and dark leafy greens with a sandwich, and so on.
3. Don't forget the fruit bowl. Place a fruit bowl on your counter to incorporate more fruit into your diet.
4. Add more fruit to your cereals. You can use a variety of fruits with your cereals, such as peaches, nectarines, and bananas. Dried fruit is another great choice.
5. Add more vegetables and herbs to your egg dishes. Add vegetables such as zucchini, onions, spinach, and tomatoes to your egg dishes (such as frittatas, muffins, and scrambled eggs).
6. Add veggies to your pasta: Pasta dishes are perfect for adding fresh vegetables and herbs.

7. Consume more vegetable soup. Start your meal with a vegetable soup. It will help you consume more veggies.
8. Add whole grains to your soups and stews. Whole grains are full of fiber and other nutrients, and help with weight loss. Add pearl barley or whole-wheat pasta to your soups and stews.
9. Add beans to your meals. It is beneficial to add beans to your every meal.

Chapter 8: Tips for the Beginners

1. Eliminate fast foods. Eliminate fast foods and choose only Mediterranean dishes.
1. Swap fats. Avoid butter and use olive oil in your cooking. Other good fats are avocados, olives, sunflower seeds, and nuts.
2. Reduce your red meat consumption and eat in smaller amounts. Mostly eat lean protein such as fish twice a week, and poultry in moderation.
3. Eat lots of vegetables. Also, consume more legumes.
4. Eat some dairy and eggs. Moderate consumption of dairy products provides health benefits. Consume Greek yogurt and cheeses. Garnish your meals with dairy.
5. Eat seafood and fish twice a week.
6. Don't drink your calories. Avoid sugar-sweetened drinks. Drink more water and an occasional glass of red wine.
7. Snack on nuts.
8. Eat pasta. Combine high-fiber vegetables and olive oil with whole grain pasta.
9. Share meals. This goes well with the Mediterranean diet idea.

10. Eat fresh fruit as dessert.
11. Amp up seasonings. Add a lot of garlic and herbs to your meals.

Chapter 9: Meal Planning

Meal planning is the key to staying on track with your nutritional goals. A popular quote from Benjamin Franklin, "When you fail to plan, you plan to fail." Choose one day or night of the week to write out everything you want to eat the following week. Plan your meals then create a grocery list according to your meals. Shop from your list so you don't stray from your plan. If you are really busy during weekdays then you can cook several meals on your weekend, freeze them and eat them during busy weekdays. Meal planning is important for several reasons:

- o Meal planning ensures that you are using your time wisely and have everything you need on hand.
- o It makes cooking easier during the week because you already know what you are going to cook.
- o Planning can help you save money.

Here are a few meal planning tips:

- o Make a big batch of quinoa in a rice cooker or on the stove top. You can use quinoa in a lot of dishes like rice. Cooking a batch ahead of time makes it easy to add a scoop to salads, stews, soups, and wraps.
- o Wash and chop vegetables like carrots and celery as soon as you get home from the grocery store. They

keep well in an airtight container in the refrigerator for 7 to 10 days and you can use them as a base for soups and sauces.

- If saving money is one of your goals then you can purchase frozen produce instead of fresh fruits and vegetables. Frozen vegetables are delicious in stir-fries and don't require any washing or chopping.
- Roast a big batch of vegetables all at once. Green beans, broccoli, and sweet potatoes are great choices to roast ahead of time. You can add them to your salads, sandwiches, wraps, and tacos.
- You can cook a whole turkey or chicken and use them in a variety of dishes such as a casserole, soup, patties, stir-fry, salads, and sandwiches.

7-Day Meal Planning
[correction: Open-Faced Greek Omelet]

Weekly Meal Planner

	Breakfast	Lunch	Dinner	Side Dishes & Snacks	Dessert
Sunday	Open Faced Greek Omelet	Mediterranean Style Stuffed Peppers	Baked Salmon with Garlic Cilantro Sauce	Mediterranean Feta Cheese Dip	No Bake Dessert Bars

	Breakfast	Lunch	Dinner	Appetizers and Snacks	Dessert
Monday	Shakshuka	Mediterranean Chicken Thighs	Greek Baked Meatballs	Garlic Brussels Sprouts	Greek Honey Cake
Tuesday	Breakfast Egg Muffins	Greek Shrimp with Tomato and Feta	Spanish Chickpea Stew	Hummus	Honey Bun Cinnamon Cookies
Wednesday	Mediterranean-Style Breakfast Toast	Moroccan Lamb Stew	Butternut Squash with Lentils and Quinoa	Baba Ganoush	Basbousa
Thursday	Egg Casserole	Mediterranean Blackened Salmon with Salsa	Lemon Garlic Shrimp with Peas and Artichokes	Mediterranean Party Platter	French Pear Tart
Friday	Mediterranean Breakfast Hash	Garlic Herb Roast Turkey	Mediterranean Baked Fish with Tomatoes and Capers	Avocado Hummus and Salsa Verde	Baklava
Saturday	Italian-Style Breakfast Strata	Greek Turkey Meatball Gyro with Tzatziki	Egyptian Style Potato Casserole	Baked Brie with Jam and Nuts	Roasted Peaches and Greek Yogurt Crostini

Chapter 10: Breakfast Recipes

Shakshuka

Prep time: 10 minutes	Cook time: 20 minutes	Servings: 6

Ingredients

- Extra virgin olive oil – 3 tbsp.
- Yellow onion – 1 large, chopped
- Green peppers – 2, chopped
- Garlic – 2 cloves, chopped
- Ground coriander – 1 tsp.
- Sweet paprika – 1 tsp.
- Ground cumin – ½ tsp.
- Red pepper flakes – 1 pinch
- Salt and pepper to taste
- Ripe tomatoes – 6, chopped
- Tomato sauce – ½ cup
- Sugar – 1 tsp.
- Eggs – 6
- Chopped fresh parsley leaves – ¼ cup
- Chopped fresh mint leaves – ¼ cup

Method
1. Heat oil in a skillet.
2. Add onions, salt, pepper, spices, garlic, and green peppers.
3. Stir-fry for 10 minutes, or until vegetables are softened.
4. Add sugar, tomatoes, and sauce.
5. Simmer for 10 to 12 minutes or until the mixture begins to reduce. Taste and adjust seasoning.
6. Make 6 "wells" in the mixture with a spoon.
7. Crack an egg on each well.
8. Lower the heat, cover and cook on low heat until the egg whites are set.
9. Uncover and sprinkle with mint and parsley.
10. Serve.

Nutritional Facts Per Serving
- Calories: 154
- Fat: 7.8g
- Carb: 14.1g
- Protein: 9g

Breakfast Egg Muffins

| Prep time: 15 minutes | Cook time: 25 minutes | Servings: 12 |

Ingredients
- Extra virgin olive oil for brushing
- Red bell pepper – 1, chopped
- Cherry tomatoes – 12, halved
- Shallot – 1, finely chopped
- Pitted Kalamata olives – 6 to 10, chopped
- Cooked chicken or turkey – 3 to 4 oz. boneless, shredded
- Chopped fresh parsley – ½ cup
- Crumbled feta to taste
- Eggs – 8
- Salt and pepper to taste
- Spanish paprika – ½ tsp.
- Ground turmeric – ¼ tsp.

Method
1. Place a rack in the center and preheat the oven to 350F.
2. Grease a nonstick 12-cup muffin pan with olive oil.
3. Mix crumbled feta, parsley, chicken, olives, shallots, tomatoes, and peppers in a bowl. Add the mixture evenly to 12 cups.

4. Whisk eggs, spices, salt, and pepper in a bowl.
5. Pour egg mixture evenly over each cup. Each cup should be about ¾ full.
6. Place muffin pan on a sheet pan.
7. Bake in the oven until egg muffins are set, about 25 minutes.
8. Cool and serve.

Nutritional Facts Per Serving
- Calories: 67
- Fat: 4.7g
- Carb: 1.2g
- Protein: 4.6g

Mediterranean-Style Breakfast Toast

| Prep time: 10 minutes | Cook time: 0 minute | Servings: 4 |

Ingredients
- Whole grain bread of choice – 4 thick slices
- Homemade hummus – ½ cup
- Mediterranean spice blend to taste
- Baby spinach – 1 handful
- Cucumber – 1, sliced
- Roma tomatoes – 1 to 2, sliced
- Chopped olives – 2 tbsp.

- o Crumbled feta cheese to taste

Method

1. Toast bread slices.
2. Spread hummus on each slice of bread.
3. Arrange with the other ingredients and serve.

Nutritional Facts Per Serving

- o Calories: 166
- o Fat: 4.2g
- o Carb: 29.4g
- o Protein: 6.1g

Banana Walnut Bread

| Prep time: 15 minutes | Cook time: 55 minutes | Servings: 12 |

Ingredients

- o Extra virgin olive oil – 1/3 cup
- o Honey – ½ cup
- o Eggs – 2
- o Ripe bananas – 2, mashed
- o Fat-free plain yogurt – 2 tbsp.
- o Fat-free milk – ¼ cup
- o Baking soda – 1 tsp.
- o Vanilla extract – 1 tsp.

- Ground cardamom – ½ tsp.
- Ground cinnamon – ½ tsp.
- Ground nutmeg – ½ tsp.
- All-purpose flour – 1 1/3 cup
- Pitted and chopped dates – ½ cup
- Chopped walnut hearts – 1/3 cup

Method
1. Preheat the oven to 325F.
2. Whisk the honey and olive oil in a bowl.
3. Add the eggs and whisk again to combine.
4. Add the nutmeg, cinnamon, cardamom, vanilla extract, baking soda, milk, yogurt, and bananas. Whisk to mix.
5. Stir in the flour, then walnuts and dates. Combine well.
6. Grease a (5 3/4" x 3") loaf pan and pour batter into the loaf pan.
7. Bake for 55 minutes at 325F.
8. Remove from the oven and cool.
9. Slice and serve.

Nutritional Facts Per Serving
- Calories: 172
- Fat: 5.9g
- Carb: 28.8g

- Protein: 2.4g

Egg Casserole

| Prep time: 15 minutes | Cook time: 35 minutes | Servings: 6 |

Ingredients
- Chopped artichokes – 10 oz.
- Large tomato – 1, chopped
- Large shallot – 1, chopped
- Fresh parsley leaves – 1 cup, chopped
- Fresh mint leaves – 1 cup, chopped
- Crumbled feta cheese – 1 ¼ cup
- Ground Parmesan cheese – ½ cup
- Fresh toast – 6 slices, cut into ½-inch pieces
- Milk – 1 ½ cup
- Eggs – 6
- Baking powder – ½ tsp.
- Ground nutmeg – ¼ tsp.
- Hot paprika – 1 tsp.
- Salt and pepper to taste

Method
1. Preheat the oven to 375F.
2. Place cut breads in a bowl.
3. In another bowl, whisk milk, salt, pepper, paprika, nutmeg, baking powder, and eggs.

4. Pour milk mixture into the bread bowl.
5. Mix in the vegetables, cheese, and herbs.
6. Mix well and transfer to a baking dish.
7. Bake at 375F until cooked through, about 35 minutes.

Nutritional Facts Per Serving
- Calories: 353
- Fat: 16g
- Carb: 35g
- Protein: 22g

Mediterranean Breakfast Hash

Prep time: 10 minutes	Cook time: 14 minutes	Servings: 4

Ingredients
- Extra virgin olive oil – 1 ½ tbsp.
- Small yellow onion – 1, chopped
- Garlic – 2 cloves, chopped
- Russet potatoes - 2, diced
- Salt and pepper to taste
- Canned chickpeas – 1 cup, drained and rinsed
- Baby asparagus – 1 lb. chopped into ¼-inch pieces
- Ground allspice – 1 ½ tsp.
- Mediterranean spice blend – 1 tsp.

- Dried oregano – 1 tsp.
- Sweet paprika – 1 tsp.
- Coriander – 1 tsp.
- Pinch sugar
- Eggs – 4
- Water
- White vinegar – 1 tsp.
- Small red onion – 1, finely chopped
- Roma tomatoes – 2, chopped
- Crumbled feta – ½ cup
- Chopped fresh parsley – 1 cup

Method
1. Heat olive oil in a skillet.
2. Add potatoes, garlic, and onion. Season with salt and pepper.
3. Stir-fry until the potatoes are tender, about 5 to 7 minutes.
4. Add asparagus, chickpeas, spices, and more salt and pepper.
5. Stir-fry for 5 to 7 minutes more.
6. Add 1 tsp. vinegar to a pot of water and bring to a steady simmer.
7. Break eggs in a bowl and carefully slide the eggs in.
8. Cook for 3 minutes then remove and drain. Season with salt and pepper.

9. Remove the skillet from the heat.
10. Add tomatoes, red onions, feta, and parsley.
11. Top with poached eggs, and serve.

Nutritional Facts Per Serving
- Calories: 535
- Fat: 20.8g
- Carb: 34.5g
- Protein: 26.6g

Italian-Style Breakfast Strata

Prep time: 15 minutes	Cook time: 50 minutes	Servings: 12

Ingredients
- Low-fat Italian chicken sausage – ¾ lb. castings removed
- Extra virgin olive oil – ¾ cup, plus 1 tbsp.
- Chopped yellow onion - 1 cup
- Chopped bell peppers – 2 cups
- Celery – 2 ribs, chopped
- Dried oregano – 1 tsp.
- Salt and black pepper
- Sundried tomato bits – ½ cup
- Parsley – ½ cup, chopped

- Canned diced tomato – 2/3 cup
- Eggs – 6
- Skim milk – ¾ cup
- Butter- 2 tbsp.
- Fillo Dough – 16 sheets, thawed
- Grated Parmesan cheese – ½ cup

Method

1. To make the filling: Sauté sausage until browned in a skillet. Break up bigger chunks into smaller pieces. Transfer to a bowl and set aside.
2. Heat olive oil in the skillet and sauté celery, peppers, and onions for 4 minutes.
3. Season with salt and pepper and add dried oregano. Transfer to the sausage bowl.
4. Now add the diced tomato, parsley, and tomato bits to the bowl and mix well.
5. In another bowl, whisk milk and eggs, and set aside.
6. Preheat the oven to 350F.
7. Melt the butter in the microwave and add ¾-cup olive oil and mix.
8. Grease a baking pan (9" x 13") with the oil-butter mixture.
9. Line the baking pan with 1 fillo sheet. Brush with oil-butter mixture and repeat with the next 7 sheets.
10. Sprinkle the last sheet with Parmesan.

11. Brush the next 8 sheets with oil-butter mixture and layer on top.
12. Spread the filling evenly on top of the sheets.
13. Pour in the milk-egg mixture and fold the excess fillo.
14. Bake for 30 to 40 minutes at 350F.
15. Remove and cool for 5 minutes.
16. Cut into squares and serve.

Nutritional Facts Per Serving
- Calories: 373
- Fat: 27.6g
- Carb: 21g
- Protein: 11.9g

Open-Faced Greek Omelet

| Prep time: 5 minutes | Cook time: 15 minutes | Servings: 4 |

Ingredients
- Extra virgin olive oil – 2 tbsp.
- Large tomato – 1, sliced
- Garlic – 1 clove, minced
- Crumbled Greek feta cheese – 2 tbsp.
- Eggs – 7
- Chopped mint leaves – 1 tbsp.
- Baking powder – ½ tsp.

- Sweet paprika – ½ tsp.
- Dill weed – ½ tsp.
- Coriander – ½ tsp.
- Salt and black pepper

Method
1. Heat olive oil in a skillet.
2. Add tomato slices and garlic.
3. Cook for 5 minutes, or until tomatoes are soft. Add feta.
4. Meanwhile, in a bowl, whisk the eggs with salt, pepper, mint, and baking powder.
5. Pour the egg mixture over the tomatoes.
6. Cover and cook until top begins to set.
7. Place the skillet to an oven and broil briefly or until fully cooked.
8. Slice the omelet into pieces.
9. Serve.

Nutritional Facts Per Serving
- Calories: 179
- Fat: 13g
- Carb: 3.4g
- Protein: 11.8g

Crust-less Zucchini Quiche

| Prep time: 10 minutes | Cook time: 35 minutes | Servings: 8 |

Ingredients
- Tomato – 1, sliced
- Extra virgin olive oil – 2 tbsp.
- Zucchini – 1, sliced
- Shallots – 3, sliced
- Salt and pepper
- Sweet Spanish paprika – 1 tsp. divided
- Part-skim shredded mozzarella – ½ cup
- Grated Parmesan – 2 tbsp.
- Eggs – 3, beaten
- Skim milk – 2/3 cup
- Baking powder – ¼ tsp.
- White whole wheat flour – ½ cup, sifted
- Fresh parsley – ¼ cup

Method
1. Preheat the oven to 350F.
2. Season the sliced tomatoes with salt. Set aside for a few minutes, then pat dry.
3. Heat oil in a skillet.
4. Add shallots, zucchini. Season with ½ tsp. paprika, salt, and pepper.

5. Stir-fry until vegetables are tender.
6. Grease a 9-inch pie dish and transfer the vegetable mixture to it.
7. Arrange sliced tomatoes on top.
8. Add mozzarella and Parmesan.
9. In a bowl, whisk milk, eggs, baking powder, flour, parsley, and ½ tsp. paprika.
10. Pour the egg mixture on top of the cheeses.
11. Bake for 30 minutes at 350F.
12. Remove and cool.
13. Slice and serve.

Nutritional Facts Per Serving
- Calories: 145
- Fat: 5.6g
- Carb: 16.5g
- Protein: 8.4g

Chapter 11: Lunch Recipes

Mediterranean-Style Stuffed Peppers

Prep time: 15 minutes	Cook time: 50 minutes	Servings: 6

Ingredients
- Extra virgin olive oil – 1 tbsp.
- Yellow onion – 1, chopped
- Ground beef – ½ lb.
- Salt and pepper
- Allspice – ½ tsp.
- Garlic powder – ½ tsp.
- Cooked or canned chickpeas – 1 cup
- Chopped parsley – ½ cup, more for garnish
- Short grain rice – 1 cup, soaked for 15 minutes, then drained
- Hot or sweet paprika – ½ tsp.
- Tomato sauce – 3 tbsp.
- Water – 2 ¼ cup
- Bell peppers – 6, tops removed, cored
- Chicken broth – ¾ cup

Method
1. Heat oil in a pot and sauté onions until golden.

2. Add meat and cook until deeply browned.
3. Season with garlic powder, allspice, salt, and pepper.
4. Stir in the chickpeas and cook briefly.
5. Now add the tomato sauce, paprika, rice, and parsley. Stir to mix.
6. Add water and simmer until liquid has reduced by one half.
7. Lower the heat and cook until rice is fully cooked, about 15 to 20 minutes.
8. Meanwhile, heat a gas grill to medium-high heat.
9. Grill bell pepper for 10 to 15 minutes, covered.
10. Turn the peppers occasionally so all sides are charred. Remove and cool.
11. Preheat the oven to 350F.
12. Fill a baking dish with ¾-cup broth and arrange the bell peppers on it.
13. Fill the bell peppers with cooked rice stuffing.
14. Cover the dish with foil.
15. Bake at 350F for 20 to 30 minutes.
16. Remove and garnish with parsley.
17. Serve.

Nutritional Facts Per Serving
- Calories: 281
- Fat: 4.8g
- Carb: 44.4g
- Protein: 14.5g

Mediterranean Chicken Thighs

| Prep time: 10 minutes | Cook time: 1 hour | Servings: 4 |

Ingredients
- Chicken thighs – 8, rinsed and pat dried
- Salt and pepper
- Olive oil – 3 tbsp. divided
- Potatoes – 1 ½ pounds, cut into small chunks
- Cherry tomatoes – 1 pint
- Roasted red peppers – 1 (10 oz.) jar, drained and sliced
- Capers – ¼ cup, drained
- Garlic – 8 cloves, crushed
- Fresh oregano – 5 sprigs
- Finely chopped parsley – 3 tbsp.

Method
1. Preheat the oven to 400F.
2. Season the chicken with salt and pepper.
3. Add oil to a roasting pan and sear the chicken until lightly golden (skin-side down).
4. Flip chicken over and turn off the heat.
5. Stir in oregano, garlic, capers, red peppers, tomatoes, and potatoes.
6. Season with salt and pepper, and drizzle with more oil.

7. Cook in the oven for 45 to 55 minutes.

Nutritional Facts Per Serving
- Calories: 481
- Fat: 20.1g
- Carb: 37.1g
- Protein: 39.1g

Greek Shrimp with Tomato and Feta

Prep time: 10 minutes	Cook time: 20 minutes	Servings: 6

Ingredients
- Large shrimp – 1 ½ lb. peeled, deveined and pat dried
- Salt and black pepper
- Dry oregano – 1 ½ tsp. divided
- Dry dill weed – 1 ½ tsp. divided
- Pinch red pepper flakes
- Garlic – 6 cloves, minced, divided
- Extra virgin olive oil – 4 tbsp. divided
- Red onion – 1, chopped
- Canned diced tomato – 1 (26 oz.), some of the liquid drained
- Juice of ½ lemon

- Chopped fresh mint leaves – 1 handful
- Chopped fresh parsley leaves – 1 handful
- Crumbled Greek feta cheese – 2 to 3 oz.
- Pitted Kalamata olives – 6 or more, chopped

Method

1. Season the shrimp with ½ tsp. garlic, red pepper flakes, ½ tsp. dry dill weed, ½ tsp. dry oregano, salt, and pepper.
2. Drizzle with 2 tbsp. oil and toss to coat. Set aside.
3. Heat 2 tbsp. oil in a skillet.
4. Add remaining garlic, and chopped onion. Stir-fry until fragrant.
5. Add lemon juice, tomatoes, remaining dry oregano, dill, salt, and pepper.
6. Bring to a boil, then lower the heat and simmer for 15 minutes.
7. Now add the shrimp and cook until pink, about 5 to 7 minutes.
8. Stir in parsley and mint.
9. Sprinkle with black olives and feta.
10. Serve.

Nutritional Facts Per Serving

- Calories: 190
- Fat: 5.2g

- Carb: 11.9g
- Protein: 25.9g

Moroccan Lamb Stew

Prep time: 15 minutes	Cook time: 2 hours 15 minutes	Servings: 6

Ingredients
- Extra virgin olive oil – 2 tbsp. and more if needed
- Yellow onion – 1, chopped
- Carrots – 3, cubed
- Small potatoes – 6, peeled and cubed
- Boneless leg of lamb – 2.5 lb. cut into cubes
- Garlic – 3 cloves, chopped
- Dried apricots – ½ cup
- Cinnamon – 1 stick
- Bay leaf – 1
- Ground allspice – 1 ½ tsp.
- Moroccan spice blend – 1 tsp. (ras el hanout)
- Ground ginger – ½ tsp.
- Plum tomatoes – 6, from a can, cut in halves
- Low-sodium beef broth – 2 ½ cups
- Chickpeas – 1 (15-oz.) can

Method
1. Heat 2 tbsp. olive oil in a Dutch oven.
2. Add potatoes, carrots, and onions, and sauté for 4 to 5 minutes.
3. Season with salt and pepper and add the garlic.
4. Remove the mixture from the pot and set aside.
5. Add more oil if needed and deeply brown the lamb on all sides. Season with salt and pepper.
6. Return the vegetables to the pot.
7. Add spices, bay leaf, cinnamon, and apricots. Mix.
8. Add broth and plum tomatoes, boil for 5 minutes.
9. Cover the pot and cook for 1 ½ hour in an oven at 350F. Check after 1 hour if the mixture needs more broth or water.
10. Stir in chickpeas and cook in the oven for 30 minutes.
11. Remove from the oven and serve.

Nutritional Facts Per Serving
- Calories: 502
- Fat: 9.7g
- Carb: 65.4 g
- Protein: 43.5g

Mediterranean Blackened Salmon with Salsa

| Prep time: 15 minutes | Cook time: 5 minutes | Servings: 4 |

Ingredients
- Cherry tomatoes – 2 cups, chopped
- Seeds of 1 large pomegranate
- Bell pepper – ½, chopped
- Shallot – 1, chopped
- Fresh mint leaves – 10 to 15, chopped
- Fresh parsley – 1 handful, chopped
- Salt and pepper
- Juice of ½ lemon
- Extra virgin olive oil – 1 tbsp.

For Salmon
- Ground cumin – 1 tsp.
- Ground coriander – 1 tsp.
- Sweet Spinach paprika – ¾ tsp.
- Aleppo pepper – ½ tsp.
- Garlic powder – ½ tsp.
- Cayenne pepper – ½ tsp.
- Salmon fillet with skin – 1 ½ lb. pat dry
- Salt and pepper
- Extra virgin olive oil as needed

Method
1. To make the salsa: combine salsa ingredients in a bowl. Mix and set aside.
2. Place oven rack about 6 inches below broiler element and preheat the broiler.
3. In a bowl, stir together all the spices.
4. Season salmon with salt and pepper.
5. Then rub the flesh with spice mixture.
6. Grease a sheet pan and place salmon.
7. Broil salmon for about 5 minutes in the oven or until the salmon reaches 115 to 125F.
8. If the salmon is not cooked enough, bake the salmon at 425F for 1 to 2 minutes.
9. Meanwhile, grill lemon halves in a skillet until browned.
10. Serve salmon with salsa. Drizzle lemon juice on top.

Nutritional Facts Per Serving
- Calories: 390
- Fat: 19.6g
- Carb: 16.5g
- Protein: 40.5g

Garlic Herb Roast Turkey

| Prep time: 30 minutes | Cook time: 45 minutes | Servings: 4 |

Ingredients
- Bone-in turkey breast – 2 ½ lb. pat dried
- Salt to taste
- Ground allspice - 1 tsp.
- Paprika – 1 tsp.
- Ground black pepper – 1 tsp.
- Nutmeg – ½ tsp.
- Garlic – 1 head, minced
- Chopped fresh parsley – 1 handful
- Extra virgin olive oil – ½ cup plus more
- Small shallots – 7 to 8, halved
- Celery – 7 sticks, chopped

For grapes
- Seedless red grapes – 1 lb.
- Extra virgin olive oil as needed
- Salt to taste

Method
1. Season the turkey with salt and pepper on both sides, including underneath the skin.
2. Preheat the oven to 450F.

3. Add grapes to a (9 1/2" x 13") baking pan.
4. Drizzle with a bit of oil and season with salt.
5. Roast in the oven for 15 minutes. Then set aside in a bowl.
6. Mix spices in a bowl. Season turkey with the spice mixture, including underneath the skin.
7. In a large bowl, combine ½-cup olive oil, garlic, and parsley.
8. Add turkey into the bowl and coat well. Also, apply the mixture underneath the skin.
9. Add celery and shallots to the previous skillet. Drizzle with olive oil and season with salt.
10. Place turkey breast on top.
11. Position oven rack to the bottom third in the preheated oven. Place the pan with the turkey.
12. Roast at 350F until turkey reaches 165F, about 45 minutes.
13. Check the turkey after 30 minutes. If it is getting too dark, cover with foil and continue to roast.
14. Add grapes back at the last 5 minutes of roasting.
15. Remove the turkey from the oven and rest for 20 minutes.
16. Slice and serve.

Nutritional Facts Per Serving
- Calories: 328

- Fat: 23.1g
- Carb: 26g
- Protein: 7.4g

Greek Roasted Vegetables (BRIAM)

Prep time: 20 minutes	Cook time: 75 minutes	Servings: 6

Ingredients
- Gold potatoes – 1 ¼ lb. peeled and thinly sliced
- Zucchini squash – 1 ¼ lb. thinly sliced
- Salt and pepper
- Dried oregano – 2 tsp.
- Dried rosemary – 1 tsp.
- Chopped parsley – ½ cup
- Garlic – 4 cloves, minced
- Extra virgin olive oil
- Canned diced tomatoes with juice – 1 (28-oz.) can
- Large red onion – 1, thinly sliced

Method
1. Place a rack in the middle and preheat the oven to 400F.
2. In a bowl, place sliced zucchini and potatoes. Season with rosemary, oregano, salt, and pepper.

3. Add a generous drizzle olive oil, parsley, and garlic. Toss to coat well.
4. Pour ½ of the canned diced tomatoes on a large skillet. Spread to cover the bottom.
5. Arrange the coated zucchini, potatoes, and sliced onions in the pan (over the tomatoes).
6. Top with the remaining diced tomatoes from the can.
7. Cover the pan with foil and bake in the oven for 45 minutes at 400F.
8. Then remove the foil and roast uncovered until veggies are cooked, about 30 to 40 minutes.
9. Remove from the oven, cool and serve.

Nutritional Facts Per Serving
- Calories: 68
- Fat: 2.6g
- Carb: 10.6g
- Protein: 1.7g

Moroccan Chicken

| Prep time: 20 minutes | Cook time: 45 minutes | Servings: 4 |

Ingredients for the spice rub
- All-natural Ras El Hanout – 1 ½ tbsp.
- Ground cinnamon – 1 ½ tsp.

- Sweet paprika – 1 tsp.
- Ground ginger – 1 tsp.
- Black pepper – ½ to 1 tsp.

For the chicken
- Whole chicken – 3 ½ lb. cut into 7 to 8 pieces
- Kosher salt
- Extra virgin olive oil – 2 tbsp. and more if needed
- Yellow onion – 1, chopped
- Garlic – 4 cloves, minced
- Chopped fresh cilantro – 1 oz.
- Lemon – 1 thinly sliced
- Pitted green olives – ¾ cup
- Raisins – ¼ cup
- Chopped dry apricots – ¼ cup
- Tomato paste – 3 tbsp.
- Low-medium chicken broth – 1 ½ cup
- Toasted slivered almonds

Method
1. Combine the Hanout and remaining spices to make a rub.
2. Season the chicken pieces with salt then rub with the spice mixture. Remember to rub underneath the skin. Cover and marinate for 2 hours or overnight in the refrigerator.

3. Heat 2 tbsp. olive oil in a 12-inch deep pan.
4. Add chicken (skin side down) and brown for 5 minutes. Then flip and brown the other side for 5 minutes.
5. Lower heat and add cilantro, garlic, and onions. Cover and cook for 3 minutes.
6. Then add dried apricots, raisins, olives, and lemon slices.
7. Mix the chicken broth and tomato paste in a bowl, then pour the mixture on top of the chicken.
8. Increase heat and simmer for 5 minutes. Then cover and cook on medium-low heat until chicken is tender and cooked through, about 30 to 45 minutes.
9. Garnish with toasted almonds and fresh cilantro.
10. Serve.

Nutritional Facts Per Serving
- Calories: 374
- Fat: 21.5g
- Carb: 16.3g
- Protein: 31.1g

Greek Turkey Meatball Gyro with Tzatziki

| Prep time: 10 minutes | Cook time: 16 minutes | Servings: 4 |

Ingredients for turkey meatball
- Ground turkey – 1 lb.
- Finely diced red onion – ¼ cup
- Garlic – 2 cloves, minced
- Oregano – 1 tsp.
- Chopped fresh spinach – 1 cup
- Salt and pepper to taste
- Olive oil – 2 tbsp.

Tzatziki Sauce
- Plain Greek yogurt – ½ cup
- Grated cucumber – ¼ cup
- Lemon juice – 2 tbsp.
- Dry dill – ½ tsp.
- Garlic powder – ½ tsp.
- Salt to taste
- Thinly sliced red onion – ½ cup
- Diced tomato – 1 cup
- Diced cucumber – 1 cup
- Whole wheat flatbreads – 4

Method
1. In a bowl, add fresh spinach, salt, pepper, oregano, garlic, red onion, and ground turkey. Mix well. Then form 1-inch balls with the mixture.
2. Heat olive oil in a skillet.
3. Add the meatballs and cook until browned on all sides, about 3 to 4 minutes per side. Remove and set aside.
4. Meanwhile, in a bowl, add lemon juice, salt, garlic powder, dill, cucumber, and yogurt. Mix well.
5. Assemble the gyros on flatbreads.
6. Top with sauce and serve.

Nutritional Facts Per Serving (1 flatbread and 3 meatballs)
- Calories: 429
- Fat: 19g
- Carb: 38g
- Protein: 28g

Chapter 12: Dinner Recipes

Baked Salmon with Garlic Cilantro Sauce

| Prep time: 5 minutes | Cook time: 10 minutes | Servings: 6 |

Ingredients for the sauce
- Garlic cloves – 4 to 6, chopped
- Salt
- Cilantro – 1 whole bunch, stems trimmed
- Extra virgin olive oil – ½ cup
- Juice of 1 lime

For the salmon
- Skinless salmon fillet – 2 lb.
- Salt and pepper
- Large tomato – 1 large, sliced
- Lime – ½, sliced

Method
1. Preheat the oven to 425F.
2. Blend all the sauce ingredients in a food processor to make a sauce.
3. Grease a baking pan and place salmon fillet on it. Sprinkle with salt and pepper.
4. Coat the salmon with sauce.

5. Arrange the lime and tomato slices on top of the salmon fillet.
6. Bake in the oven for 10 to 12 minutes at 425F.
7. Then remove and cover loosely with foil.
8. Bake another 8 minutes more.
9. Serve.

Nutritional Facts Per Serving
- Calories: 302
- Fat: 16.7g
- Carb: 5.4g
- Protein: 34.4g

Greek Baked Meatballs

Prep time: 20 minutes	Cook time: 1 hour	Servings: 8 (16 meatballs)

Ingredients
- Whole wheat bread – 2 slices, toasted
- Milk – ¼ to 1/3 cup
- Lean ground beef – 1.5 lb.
- Small yellow onion – 1, chopped
- Garlic – 3 cloves, minced
- Eggs – 2

- Ground cumin – 1 tsp.
- Ground cinnamon – ½ tsp.
- Dried oregano – ½ tsp.
- Chopped fresh parsley – ½ cup
- Salt and pepper
- Extra virgin olive oil for drizzling

For the red sauce
- Extra virgin olive oil – 2 tbsp.
- Yellow onion – 1, chopped
- Garlic – 2 cloves, minced
- Dry red wine – ½ cup
- Canned tomato sauce – 30 oz.
- Bay leaf – 1
- Ground cumin – ¾ tsp.
- Cinnamon – ½ tsp.
- Sugar – ½ tsp.
- Salt and pepper

Method
1. Add the toasted bread in a bowl and cover with milk to soak. Once soaked completely, squeeze the milk out and discard the milk.
2. In a bowl, add beef, remaining meatball ingredients and soaked bread.

3. Knead to combine. Cover and set aside in the refrigerator.
4. Preheat the oven to 400F.
5. Meanwhile, prepare the sauce: heat oil in a skillet.
6. Add onions and cook for 3 minutes.
7. Add garlic and cook for 1 minute more.
8. Add red wine and cook until reduced by half.
9. Add bay leaf, tomato sauce, and remaining sauce ingredients.
10. Bring to a boil, then lower the heat and simmer for 15 minutes.
11. Grease a large baking dish with olive oil.
12. Remove the meat mixture from the refrigerator.
13. Wet your hands and make large meatballs. You should get about 15 to 16 meatballs.
14. Arrange the meatballs in the baking dish and top with the sauce.
15. Bake in the middle rack of the oven until the meatballs are cooked through, about 40 to 45 minutes. Check once and add water if needed.
16. Remove and drizzle with olive oil.
17. Garnish with parsley and serve.

Nutritional Facts Per Meatball
- Calories: 64
- Fat: 2.7g

- Carb: 7.5g
- Protein: 2.2g

Spanish Chickpea Stew

Prep time: 15 minutes	Cook time: 25 minutes	Servings: 8

Ingredients
- Extra virgin olive oil – 1 tbsp. plus more as needed
- Baby spinach – 10 oz.
- Blanched almonds – 2 ½ oz.
- Whole wheat bread – 2 slices (crust removed, and cut into small cubes)
- Garlic – 3 cloves, minced
- Ground cumin – 1 ¼ tsp.
- Smoked paprika – ½ tsp.
- Cayenne pepper – ½ tsp.
- Salt and pepper
- Sherry vinegar – 2 tbsp.
- Small onion – 1, chopped
- Sweet bell pepper – 1 small, cored and chopped
- Canned chickpeas – 1 lb. drained and rinsed
- Tomato sauce – ½ cup

For garnish
- Toasted blanched almonds
- Cubed bread, toasted in olive oil
- Fresh cilantro leaves

Method
1. Heat oil in a skillet.
2. Add spinach and stir-fry until wilted. Remove from heat and drain.
3. Add more oil to the skillet and add bread and almonds.
4. Sauté until almonds are golden brown.
5. Add spices, garlic, salt and pepper.
6. Cook until the garlic is colored.
7. Cool the mixture then add to a food processor.
8. Add vinegar and pulse until paste-like. Set aside.
9. Clean the skillet and add a bit more oil.
10. Add bell pepper and onion, and stir-fry until tender.
11. Add ½-cup water, tomato sauce, and chickpeas. Season with salt and pepper.
12. Bring to a boil, then lower heat and simmer for 10 minutes.
13. Add the bread mixture and wilted spinach to the chickpeas.
14. Stir and simmer for 5 minutes. Taste and adjust seasoning.

15. Add a splash of vinegar. Garnish with toasted almonds, toasted bread, and cilantro.
16. Drizzle with olive oil and serve.

Nutritional Facts Per Serving
- Calories: 192
- Fat: 8g
- Carb: 24.2g
- Protein: 7.6g

Butternut Squash with Lentils and Quinoa

Prep time: 20 minutes	Cook time: 25 minutes	Servings: 8

Ingredients
- Small whole butternut squash – 1, peeled and cubed
- Salt to taste
- Ground cinnamon – 2 tsp. divided
- Allspice – 2 tsp. divided
- Coriander – 1 tsp. divided
- Paprika – 1 tsp. divided
- Cumin – ¾ tsp.
- Garlic – 6 cloves, peeled
- Extra virgin olive oil

- Dry quinoa – 1 cup, soaked a few minutes, then rinsed
- Dry black lentils – 1 cup, sorted and rinsed
- Water
- Scallions – 2, white and green parts, trimmed and chopped
- Fresh parsley – 1 handful, chopped
- Fresh lemon juice
- Tooted slivered almond – ½ cup

Method

1. Preheat the oven to 425F.
2. Place cubed butternut squash on a large baking sheet.
3. Season with ¼ tsp. cumin, ½ tsp. paprika, ½ tsp. coriander, 1 tsp. allspice, 1 tsp. cinnamon, and salt.
4. Drizzle with olive oil and toss.
5. Spread the squash evenly and bake in the milled rack for 15 minutes. Then remove from heat, add garlic and drizzle with more oil. Toss and bakefor another 10 minutes.
6. Meanwhile, make the quinoa and lentils.
7. Add 3 cups water and lentils in a pan. Season with salt and bring to a boil.
8. Then lower heat and simmer for 20 to 25 minutes. Drain.
9. Cook quinoa at the same time according to package instructions.

10. Place cooked quinoa and lentils in a large bowl. Season with salt and remaining spices. Toss to combine. Add the cooked butternut squash.
11. Add scallions, fresh parsley, and chopped garlic.
12. Toss to mix. Drizzle with lemon juice, and olive oil.
13. Toss again to mix. Top with toasted almonds and serve.

Nutritional Facts Per Serving
- Calories: 245
- Fat: 6.5g
- Carb: 38.3g
- Protein: 11g

Lemon Garlic Shrimp with Peas and Artichokes

Prep time: 10 minutes	Cook time: 20 minutes	Servings: 4

Ingredients
- Ground coriander – 1 ½ tsp.
- Ground cumin – 1 ½ tsp.
- Aleppo-style pepper – 1 tsp.
- Sweet Spinach paprika – 1 tsp.

For shrimp
- Large shrimps or prawns – 1 lb. (peeled, deveined, tail on)
- Salt and pepper
- Extra virgin olive oil – 2 tbsp.
- Small onion – 1, sliced
- Garlic cloves – 6 to 8, chopped
- Dry white wine – 1 cup
- Fresh lemon juice – 2 tbsp.
- Honey – 2 tsp.
- Chicken broth - ½ cup
- Frozen peas – 1 ½ cup, thawed
- Baby artichokes – 1 (15-oz.) can, drained
- Grated Parmesan cheese to taste
- Fresh chopped parsley for garnish

Method
1. Mix the spices in a bowl.
2. Place shrimp in another bowl and season with salt and about 2 ½ tsp. of the spice mixture. Set shrimp aside.
3. Heat 2 tbsp. olive oil in a skillet.
4. Add onions and stir-fry for 5 minutes.
5. Add garlic and stir-fry for 1 to 2 minutes more. Don't brown.
6. Add white wine and heat until reduced by half.

7. Then add broth, honey, and lemon juice. Raise heat and bring the mixture to a boil.
8. Add artichokes and peas. Season with salt and pepper, and remaining spices.
9. Cook until peas are cooked through, about 10 minutes.
10. Add shrimp and cook until just pink.
11. Remove from heat and garnish with fresh parsley and Parmesan.
12. Serve.

Nutritional Facts Per Serving
- Calories: 323
- Fat: 8.9g
- Carb: 24.7g
- Protein: 29.8g

Mediterranean Baked Fish with Tomatoes and Capers

| Prep time: 5 minutes | Cook time: 30 minutes | Servings: 6 |

Ingredients
- Extra virgin olive oil – 1/3 cup
- Small red onion – 1, finely chopped
- Large tomatoes – 2, diced
- Garlic – 10 cloves, chopped

- Ground coriander – 1 ½ tsp.
- All-natural sweet Spanish paprika – 1 tsp.
- Organic ground cumin – 1 tsp.
- Cayenne pepper – ½ tsp.
- Capers – 1 ½ tbsp.
- Salt and pepper
- Golden raisins – 1/3 cup
- Whitefish fillet – 1 ½ lb.
- Juice of ½ lemon
- Zest of 1 lemon
- Fresh parsley

Method
1. Heat olive oil over medium heat in a saucepan.
2. Add onions and stir-fry until gold in color, about 3 minutes.
3. Add raisins, capers, pepper, salt, spices, garlic, and tomatoes.
4. Bring to boil, lower heat and simmer for 15 minutes or so.
5. Heat oven to 400F.
6. Season the fish with salt and pepper on both sides.
7. Into the bottom of a 9 1/2" x 13" baking dish, pour ½ of the cooked tomato sauce.
8. Arrange the fish on top, add lemon juice and jest. Top with the remaining tomato sauce.

9. Bake at 400F for 15 to 18 minutes, or until fish is cooked.
10. Remove from the heat and garnish with parsley.
11. Serve.

Nutritional Facts Per Serving
- Calories: 308
- Fat: 17.4g
- Carb: 13.3g
- Protein: 27g

Greek-Style Braised Eggplant

Prep time: 20 minutes	Cook time: 55 minutes	Servings: 6

Ingredients
- Eggplant – 1.5 lb. cut into cubes
- Salt
- Extra virgin olive oil – ¼ cup, plus more if needed
- Yellow onion – 1 large, chopped
- Green bell pepper – 1, cored, and diced
- Carrot – 1, chopped
- Garlic – 6 cloves, minced
- Bay leaves – 2
- Sweet paprika – 1 to 1 ½ tsp.

- Ground coriander – 1 tsp.
- Dry oregano – 1 tsp.
- Ground cinnamon – ¾ tsp.
- Organic ground turmeric – ½ tsp.
- Black pepper – ½ tsp.
- Chopped tomato – 1 (28-oz.) can
- Chickpeas – 2 (15-oz.) cans, reserve the liquid
- Parsley and mint for garnish

Method
1. Heat oven to 400F.
2. Season the eggplant cubes with salt and place in a colander for 20 minutes. Then rinse with water and pat dry.
3. Heat ¼-cup olive oil in a large bruiser.
4. Add carrot, peppers, and onions.
5. Stir-fry for 2 to 3 minutes.
6. Then add salt, spices, bay leaf, and garlic. Stir-fry for 1 minute.
7. Add chickpeas with liquid, tomato, and eggplant. Stir to combine.
8. Bring to a rolling boil for 10 minutes or so. Stir often.
9. Then remove from stove top and transfer to oven.
10. Cook in the oven uncovered until eggplant is fully cooked, about 45 minutes. Check once during cooking if more liquid is needed.

11. Remove from the oven and drizzle with olive oil.
12. Garnish with herbs and serve.

Nutritional Facts Per Serving
- Calories: 438
- Fat: 5.8g
- Carb: 86g
- Protein: 19g

Egyptian-Style Potato Casserole

Prep time: 15 minutes	Cook time: 1 hour 10 minutes	Servings: 6

Ingredients for meat sauce
- Extra virgin olive oil – 2 tbsp.
- Chopped yellow onion – 1 cup
- Garlic – 3 cloves, minced
- Organic lean ground beef – 1 lb.
- Ground allspice – 1 ½ tsp.
- Coriander – 1 ½ tsp.
- Sweet Spanish paprika – ½ tsp.
- Salt and pepper
- Peeled tomato – 1 (28-oz.) can
- Water – ½ cup

For potatoes
- Gold potatoes – 1 ½ lb. peeled and cut into wedges
- Large carrots – 3, peeled and chopped
- Green bell pepper – 1, cored and sliced into strips
- Salt and pepper
- Allspice – ¾ tsp.
- Coriander – ¾ tsp.
- Water
- Chopped fresh parsley – ½ cup

Method
1. Heat oven to 375F.
2. Heat 2 tbsp. olive oil in a skillet.
3. Add onion and stir-fry until translucent.
4. Then add garlic and cook for 30 seconds.
5. Add ground meat and season with salt, pepper, and spices.
6. Stir-fry until fully browned.
7. Add water and peeled tomatoes.
8. Bring to a boil, then lower heat. Cover and simmer for 10 minutes.
9. Taste and adjust seasoning.
10. Arrange the bell peppers, carrots, and potato wedges in a 9″ x 13″ baking pan.
11. Season with coriander, allspice, salt, and pepper. Toss to combine.

12. Add ¾ cup water and top with the meat sauce.
13. Cover with foil and bake for 30 minutes. Then remove the foil and bake until potatoes are tender, about 10 to 15 minutes.
14. Remove from the oven and top with parsley.
15. Serve.

Nutritional Facts Per Serving
- Calories: 280
- Fat: 9g
- Carb: 30.6g
- Protein: 20.6g

Spanish Chicken and Rice Recipe

| Prep time: 10 minutes | Cook time: 1 hour | Servings: 4 |

Ingredients for chicken
- Medium grain rice – 1 ½ cup (soaked 15 minutes, then drained)
- Chicken thighs – 4, bone-in, skin-on (pat dry)
- Chicken drumsticks – 4, skin-on (pat dry)
- Olive oil
- Bulk chorizo sausage – 12 oz. casings removed
- Green bell pepper – 1 large, cored, chopped
- Red onion – 1 medium, peeled, and chopped

- Garlic – 2 cloves, peeled and crushed
- Large ripe tomato – 1, chopped
- Tomato sauce – 3 tbsp.
- Chicken broth – 3 cups

For the spice rub

- Smoked paprika – 1 tbsp.
- Garlic powder – 1 tsp.
- Salt – 1 tsp.
- Black pepper – 1 tsp.
- Cayenne pepper – ½ tsp.

Method

1. Mix the spice rub ingredients in a bowl.
2. Rub the chicken with the spice rub. Also, rub under the skin.
3. Heat 1 tbsp. olive oil in a deep skillet.
4. Add chicken and brown deeply on both sides. Remove and set aside.
5. Add the chorizo in a pan. Cook until browned, about 10 minutes.
6. Add the green peppers and cook another 5 minutes. Stir occasionally.
7. Add the chicken broth, tomato paste, chopped tomato, garlic, onions, and browned chicken back to the pan.

8. Bring to a boil and lower the heat to medium and cover.
9. Cook for 25 minutes.
10. Uncover and remove the chicken.
11. Stir in the rice into the cooking liquid and cook for 1 to 2 minutes, uncovered.
12. Now add the chicken back on top of the rice.
13. Lower the heat and cover the pan.
14. Cook until the rice is fully cooked, about 20 to 25 minutes.
15. Turn off the heat and keep the pan covered for 10 minutes.
16. Serve.

Nutritional Facts Per Serving
- Calories: 806
- Fat: 35.2g
- Carb: 64g
- Protein: 54.5g

Chapter 13: Appetizers and Snacks

Mediterranean Feta Cheese Dip

| Prep time: 5 minutes | Total time: 5 minutes | Servings: 6 |

Ingredients
- Feta cheese – 8 to 10 oz. crumbled
- Cream cheese – 3 oz., room temperature
- Olive oil – 3 tbsp.
- Honey – 1 tsp.
- Persian cucumber – 1, chopped
- Jalapeno – 1, chopped
- Sun-dried tomato bits – ¾ cup
- Basil leaves – 10, torn
- Chopped chives – 1 ½ tbsp.

Method
1. In a bowl, place the honey, 1 tbsp. olive oil, cream cheese, and feta. Mix to combine.
2. Add 2 tbsp. olive oil, and the remaining ingredients. Combine.
3. Transfer the feta cheese dip into a serving bowl.
4. Serve with pita chips or bread.

Nutritional Facts Per Serving
- Calories: 251

- Fat: 21.6g
- Carb: 7.6g
- Protein: 8.5g

Hummus

| Prep time: 5 minutes | Cook time: 15 minutes | Servings: 8 |

Ingredients
- Cooked chickpeas – 3 cups, peeled
- Garlic – 1 to 2 cloves, minced
- Ice cubes – 3 to 4
- Tahini paste – 1/3 cup
- Salt – ½ tsp.
- Juice of 1 lemon
- Hot water if needed
- Extra virgin olive oil
- Sumac

Method
1. Pulse minced garlic, and chickpeas in a food processor until powder-like mixture forms.
2. Keep the processor running, and add lemon juice, salt, tahini, and ice cubes. Blend for about 4 minutes. Blend until you get a smooth mixture. Add a little hot water if necessary.

3. Spread in a serving bowl and drizzle with olive oil.
4. Sprinkle sumac and enjoy with veggies or pita wedges.

Nutritional Facts Per Serving
- Calories: 176
- Fat: 8.7g
- Carb: 19.4g
- Protein: 7.2g

Baba Ganoush

Prep time: 10 minutes	Cook time: 40 minutes	Servings: 4

Ingredients
- Large eggplant – 1, cut in half
- Extra virgin olive oil
- Plain Greek yogurt – 1 tbsp.
- Tahini – 1 ½ tbsp.
- Garlic clove – 1
- Lime or lemon juice – 1 tbsp.
- Salt and pepper
- Cayenne pepper – ½ tsp. to 1 tsp.
- Sumac – ½ tsp. more for garnish
- Toasted pine nuts and parsley for garnish

Method
1. Preheat the oven to 425F.
2. Make a few slits in the skin of the eggplant.
3. Sprinkle the eggplant flesh with salt and set aside for a few minutes. Then dab dry.
4. Lightly oil a baking sheet and place the eggplant halves, flesh side down.
5. Drizzle with olive oil and bake in the oven at 425F until the eggplant fully softens, about 30 to 40 minutes. Remove from the oven and set aside to cool.
6. Scoop the flesh out and drain in a colander.
7. In a food processor, add lime juice, spices, garlic, tahini, yogurt, and eggplant flesh. Pulse to blend. Don't over blend.
8. Spread the baba ganoush in a bowl.
9. Drizzle with olive oil, sumac, pine nuts, and parsley.
10. Serve with pita bread.

Nutritional Facts Per Serving
- Calories: 287
- Fat: 27.3g
- Carb: 11.5g
- Protein: 3.3g

Mediterranean Party Platter

| Prep time: 20 minutes | Total time: 20 minutes | Servings: 12 |

Ingredients
- Baby eggplants – 2, sliced lengthwise
- Salt
- Olive oil
- Store-bought creamy hummus – 10 oz. tub (or homemade)
- Store-bought red pepper hummus – 10 oz. tub (or homemade)
- Bell pepper – ½, cored
- Store-bought or homemade tzatziki – 10 oz. tub
- Campari tomatoes – 6, quartered
- Baby cucumbers – 6, sliced into spears
- Pitted Kalamata olives
- Marinated artichoke hearts – 1 (15-oz.) can
- Greek feta cheese – 6 oz. cubed
- Baby mozzarella cheese balls – 6 oz.
- Prosciutto di Parma – 3 oz.
- California fresh figs – 6, halved
- Sumac – 1 tsp.
- Pita bread for serving

Method

1. Season the eggplant slices with salt and set aside for 20 minutes, then pat dry.
2. Preheat the oven to 400F.
3. Grease a baking pan with oil and place the eggplant slices. Drizzle with oil and roast for 20 minutes.
4. Meanwhile, assemble the remaining ingredients on a large platter.
5. When the eggplant is roasted, remove it from the oven and sprinkle with 1 tsp. sumac.
6. Enjoy with warm pita and crostini.

Nutritional Facts Per Serving
- Calories: 219
- Fat: 12.1g
- Carb: 25g
- Protein: 7.2g

Avocado Hummus and Salsa Verde

Prep time: 15 minutes	Total time: 15 minutes	Servings: 6

Ingredients for hummus
- Garlic – 2 cloves
- Chickpeas – 15 oz. can, drained
- Medium ripe avocado – 1 ½, chopped
- Greek yogurt – 2 tbsp.

- Tahini – 3 tbsp.
- Salt
- Ground cumin – ¼ tsp.
- Juice of ½ lime
- Chickpeas canning liquid
- Cayenne pepper – ¼ tsp. for garnish

For Salsa Verde
- Large tomatillos – 5, cleaned and halved
- Fresh chopped cilantro leaves – 1 packed cup
- Chopped red onions – ½ cup
- Garlic – 1 clove
- Jalapeno pepper – ½
- Salt and pepper
- Juice of ½ lime
- Olive oil – 1 tbsp.

Method
1. Pulse chickpeas, lime juice, cumin, salt, tahini, yogurt, avocado, and garlic in a food processor until smooth. Transfer to a serving bowl.
2. Garnish with cayenne pepper, cover and refrigerate.
3. Clean and dry the food processor. Add the salsa ingredients and blend until smooth.
4. Top the avocado hummus with 1/3 cup of salsa verde (drain the salsa verde before topping).

5. Place the remaining salsa to another bowl.
6. Serve with tortilla chips.

Nutritional Facts Per Serving
- Calories: 234
- Fat: 16.3g
- Carb: 19.6g
- Protein: 6.3g

Baked Brie with Jam and Nuts

Prep time: 5 minutes	Cook time: 10 minutes	Servings: 10

Ingredients
- Fig jam or honey – 3 tbsp. divided
- Dried mission figs – ¼ cup to 1/3 cup, sliced
- Shelled pistachios – ¼ to 1/3 cup, chopped
- Walnut hearts – ¼ to 1/3 cup, roughly chopped
- Round French brie – 13 oz.

Method
1. Preheat the oven to 375F.
2. Microwave the fig jam for 30 seconds to soften.
3. Combine nuts and sliced figs in a bowl.

4. Add half of the fig jam and mix well to coat the nut mixture.
5. Place the brie in a skillet and coat with the remaining jam.
6. Top brie with nut and fig mixture.
7. Place brie skillet on top of a baking sheet and bake for 10 minutes at 375F.
8. Remove and cool. Serve with crackers.

Nutritional Facts Per Serving
- Calories: 168
- Fat: 13.1g
- Carb: 6.4g
- Protein: 0.7g

Garlic Shrimp with Sauce

Prep time: 10 minutes	Cook time: 16 minutes	Servings: 4

Ingredients
- Uncooked prawns – 1.5 lb. peeled, deveined and rinsed
- Salt and pepper
- Extra virgin olive oil

Sauce

- Garlic – 1 small head, trimmed
- Chopped cilantro leaves – 1 cup
- Juice of 1 lime
- Dry white wine – 1 tbsp.
- Olive oil – 3 tbsp.
- Chili sauce – 2 tbsp.

Method

1. Preheat the oven to 400F.
2. Pat dry prawns and season with salt and pepper. Set aside in the fridge.
3. Drizzle the garlic with oil and roast in the oven for 10 to 15 minutes or until tender at 400F. Remove, peel and chop.
4. In a bowl, combine the garlic with remaining sauce ingredients. Whisk to mix and set aside.
5. Grease a grill or griddle and heat on medium-high.
6. Coat the prawns with olive oil and grill for 3 to 4 minutes on each side. Don't overcook.
7. Add the prawns in a bowl and coat with garlic sauce.
8. Serve.

Nutritional Facts Per Serving

- Calories: 380
- Fat: 25.5g
- Carb: 4.2g

- Protein: 34.7g

Phyllo Dough Meat Rolls

| Prep time: 25 minutes | Cook time: 23 minutes | Servings: 16 |

Ingredients
- Ground beef – 1 lb.
- Small yellow onion – 1, chopped
- Allspice – 1 tsp.
- Salt and pepper
- Olive oil – 1 tbsp. plus 1 cup

Filling ingredients
- Creamy feta cheese – 5 oz.
- Shredded mozzarella cheese – 1 cup
- Eggs – 2
- Dill weed – 1 tsp.
- Olive oil – 1 tbsp.

Other
- Phyllo sheets – 16 to 20
- Egg – 1, mixed with little water

Method

1. Preheat the oven to 400F.
2. In a pan, heat 1 tbsp. olive oil.
3. Add onions and stir-fry briefly.
4. Add ground beef and spices.
5. Stir-fry for 8 minutes, or until fully cooked. Set aside.
6. Add the other filling ingredients to the cooled beef.
7. Lay two sheets of phyllo on a cutting board and brush with oil.
8. Cut in the middle to make two long phyllo strips.
9. Make a roll with one phyllo strip.
10. Add the filling and roll to cover. Trim the ends.
11. Brush the finished roll with egg wash and oil, and place on a lightly oiled baking sheet. Repeat with the other phyllo roll.
12. Bake 15 minutes in the 400F oven.
13. Remove and serve warm with a dip or a sauce.

Nutritional Facts Per Serving
- Calories: 303
- Fat: 21.1g
- Carb: 16.1g
- Protein: 13g

Roasted Cauliflower with Lemon and Cumin

| Prep time: 10 minutes | Cook time: 45 minutes | Servings: 6 |

Ingredients
- Cauliflower – 1 head, cut into florets
- Extra virgin olive oil
- Ground cumin – 2 tsp.
- Harissa spice – 1 tsp.
- Salt and pepper
- Lemon juice – 1 to 2 tbsp.
- Fresh parsley for garnish
- Toasted pine nuts – ¼ cup

For Tahini Sauce
- Garlic – 1 to 2 cloves
- Salt – ½ tsp.
- Tahini paste – ½ cup
- Lemon juice – ½ cup
- Cold water – ¼ cup
- Parsley – 1 cup

Method
1. Preheat the oven to 475F.
2. Place the cauliflower florets on a baking sheet and drizzle with olive oil. Coat well.
3. In a small dish, combine harissa and cumin.
4. Season cauliflower with salt, pepper, and spice mixture. Toss to coat.

5. Cover the baking sheet with foil and roast on the middle rack of the oven for 15 minutes. Then remove the foil and roast for 30 minutes more.
6. Meanwhile, prepare the tahini sauce: mix salt and garlic and make a paste.
7. Pulse the lime juice, tahini paste, and garlic paste in a food processor. Add a bit more water and blend until smooth.
8. Remove the cauliflower from the oven and drizzle with a little tahini and lemon juice. Garnish with fresh parsley and toasted nuts.
9. Serve.

Nutritional Facts Per Serving
- Calories: 72
- Fat: 2.8g
- Carb: 11.4g
- Protein: 0.7g

Grilled Greek Pizza

Prep time: 30 minutes	Cook time: 6 minutes	Servings: 2 (12-inch pizzas)

Ingredients
- Pizza dough – 1 pound (homemade or store-bought)
- Hummus – 1 pound

- Baby arugula – 1 cup
- Pitted Greek olives – 2/3 cup
- Cherry or grape tomatoes – 2/3 cup, halved
- Crumbled feta cheese – ¼ cup
- Olive oil for drizzle

Method
1. Cut the dough in half then roll each with a rolling pin to make 12-inch circles.
2. Spread parchment paper and place the dough circles on it. Lightly oil the tops.
3. Preheat the grill to high and place the baking/grilling stone on the grill.
4. One by one, flip the dough circles onto the grill grates or stone. Grill for 2 to 3 minutes per side.
5. Then spread 8 oz. of hummus on each crust and top both with feta, olives, tomatoes, arugula, and drizzle with olive oil.
6. Serve.

Nutritional Facts Per Serving (1 pizza)
- Calories: 1060
- Fat: 39g
- Carb: 145g
- Protein: 39g

Chapter 14: Salad and Soup Recipes

Cream of Roasted Cauliflower Soup

Prep time: 15 minutes	Cook time: 60 minutes	Servings: 6

Ingredients
- Cauliflower – 2 heads – 2 cut into florets
- Greek extra virgin olive oil – 2 tbsp. plus more for drizzling
- Salt and pepper
- Small sweet onion – 1 chopped
- Garlic – 5 cloves, chopped
- Sweet Spanish paprika – 2 ½ tsp.
- Ground cumin – 2 tsp.
- Ground sumac – 1 tsp.
- Ground turmeric – ¼ tsp.
- Low-sodium vegetable broth – 4 cups
- Water – 1 cup
- Fat-free half-and-half – 2 ½ cups
- Juice of ½ lemon
- Chopped fresh dill – 1 cup

Method
1. Preheat the oven to 425F.
2. Place the cauliflower florets on a large sheet pan and season with salt and pepper, and drizzle with olive oil. Toss to coat.
3. Spread the cauliflower florets evenly and roast in the oven for 45 minutes at 425F. Turn once at the halfway mark.
4. Heat 2 tbsp. olive oil in a heavy pot.
5. Add onions and stir-fry until translucent.
6. Add spices and garlic, and stir-fry for a few seconds.
7. Add ¾ of the roasted cauliflowers and stir to coat with spices.
8. Then add the water and broth.
9. Bring to a boil and lower the heat to medium. Simmer for 5 to 7 minutes.
10. Uncover and remove from the heat. Blend with a hand mixer until smooth.
11. Return to the heat and stir in lime juice and half-and-half.
12. Then stir in the reserved cauliflower.
13. Cook briefly and adjust seasoning.
14. Stir in dill and serve.

Nutritional Facts Per Serving
- Calories: 195

- Fat: 10g
- Carb: 19.2g
- Protein: 8.5g

Mediterranean Bean Soup with Tomato Pesto

Prep time: 10 minutes	Cook time: 27 minutes	Servings: 8

Ingredients
- Extra virgin olive oil – 2 tbsp. and more if needed
- Large russet potato – 1, cubed
- Medium yellow onion – 1, chopped
- Diced tomatoes – 1 (15-oz.) can
- White vinegar – 1 tbsp.
- Ground coriander – 1 tbsp.
- Spanish paprika – 1 tsp.
- Salt and pepper
- Low sodium vegetable broth – 5 cups
- Frozen spinach – 8 oz.
- Red kidney beans – 1 (15-oz.) can
- Cannellini beans – 1 (15-oz.) can
- Chickpeas – 1 (15-oz.) can
- Basil leaves for garnish
- Toasted pine nuts – 1/3 cup, for garnish

For tomato pesto sauce
- Large garlic – 2 to 3 cloves
- Diced fresh tomatoes – 1 ½ cup
- Large basil leaves – 15 to 20
- Salt and pepper
- Extra virgin olive oil – ½ cup
- Grated Parmesan cheese – 1/3 to ½ cup

Method
1. Heat 2 tbsp. olive oil in a heavy pot.
2. Add onions and potatoes, and stir-fry for 5 minutes.
3. Add salt, pepper, spices, vinegar, and tomatoes.
4. Combine, cover and cook for 4 minutes more.
5. Add frozen spinach and vegetable broth.
6. Bring to a boil for 4 minutes.
7. Add chickpeas, cannellini beans, and kidney beans.
8. Bring back to a boil, then lower heat, cover and cook for 15 to 20 minutes more.
9. Meanwhile, make the tomato paste. Pulse tomatoes and garlic in a food processor for a few times to combine.
10. Add basil and puree. A little bit at a time, drizzle in olive oil.
11. Transfer the pesto in a bowl and stir in Parmesan.
12. Remove the soup when ready. Stir in tomato pesto.

13. Transfer to serving bowl. Top each bowl with toasted pine nuts and basil leaves.
14. Serve.

Nutritional Facts Per Serving
- Calories: 374
- Fat: 16g
- Carb: 44.4g
- Protein: 15.2g

Roasted Carrot Ginger Soup

Prep time: 10 minutes	Cook time: 55 minutes	Servings: 6

Ingredients
- Carrots – 3 lb. peeled
- Extra virgin olive oil
- Salt and pepper
- Garlic – 4 cloves, chopped
- Grated fresh ginger – 1 tsp.
- Low-sodium vegetable broth – 5 ½ cups, divided
- Ground coriander – 1 tsp.
- Allspice – 1 tsp.
- Unsweetened fat-free half-and-half - 1 ½ cup
- Fresh mint for garnish

Method
1. Preheat the oven to 425F.
2. Grease a baking sheet with oil and arrange the carrots on it.
3. Season with salt and pepper, and drizzle with olive oil.
4. Roast in the oven for 45 minutes at 425F. Turn over mid-way through.
5. Cut the carrots into chunks and place in a food processor with 3 cups broth, ginger, and garlic. Puree until smooth.
6. Add the carrot puree into a cooking pot.
7. Add allspice, remaining broth, and coriander.
8. Heat on medium heat and stir occasionally.
9. Lower the heat and stir in the heavy cream.
10. Remove from the stove and transfer to serving bowls.
11. Garnish with fresh mint leaves.

Nutritional Facts Per Serving
- Calories: 191
- Fat: 8.1g
- Carb: 28.9g
- Protein: 3.3g

Greek Lemon Chicken Soup

| Prep time: 5 minutes | Cook time: 30 minutes | Servings: 6 |

Ingredients
- Olive oil – 1 tbsp. plus more as needed
- Carrots – ½ to 1 cup, chopped
- Celery – ½ to 1 cup, chopped
- Green onions – ½ to 1 cup, chopped
- Garlic – 2 cloves, chopped
- Low-sodium chicken broth – 8 cups
- Bay leaves – 2
- Short grain rice – 1 cup
- Salt and pepper
- Cooked boneless chicken breasts – 2, shredded
- Lemon juice – ½ cup
- Eggs – 2
- Parsley

Method
1. Heat 1 tbsp. olive oil in a Dutch oven.
2. Add green onions, celery, and carrots.
3. Sauté and add in the garlic.
4. Add broth and bay leaves.
5. Bring to a boil and add salt, pepper, and rice.
6. Lower the heat and simmer until rice is tender, about 20 minutes.

7. Now stir in cooked chicken.
8. To make the sauce, whisk together eggs and lemon juice in a bowl.
9. Temper the eggs by pouring 2 ladles-full of broth from the cooking pot (while continuing to whisk).
10. Mix well and add the sauce to the chicken soup and stir to mix.
11. Garnish with parsley and serve.

Nutritional Facts Per Serving
- Calories: 247
- Fat: 8.3g
- Carb: 29.8g
- Protein: 12.3g

Tabouli Salad

Prep time: 20 minutes	Total time: 20 minutes	Servings: 6

Ingredients
- Extra fine bulgur wheat – ½ cup (soaked 5 minutes and drained very well)
- Roma tomatoes – 4, finely chopped
- English cucumber – 1, finely chopped
- Parsley – 2 bunches, finely chopped

- Mint – 12 to 15, finely chopped
- Green onions – 4, white and green parts, finely chopped
- Salt
- Lime juice – 3 to 4 tbsp.
- Extra virgin olive oil – 3 to 4 tbsp.
- Romaine lettuce leaves to serve

Method
1. Very finely chop all the herbs, vegetables and green onions and place in a bowl.
2. Add the bulgur and season with salt. Mix gently.
3. Now add the olive oil, lime juice and mix again.
4. Cover and refrigerate for 30 minutes.
5. Serve.

Nutritional Facts Per Serving
- Calories: 190
- Fat: 10g
- Carb: 25.5g
- Protein: 3.2g

Fattoush Salad

| Prep time: 20 minutes | Total time: 20 minutes | Servings: 6 |

Ingredients
- Pita bread – 2 loaves, toasted until crisp, not browned
- Extra virgin olive oil – 3 tbsp.
- Sumac – ½ tsp.
- Salt and pepper
- Romaine lettuce – 1 heart, chopped
- English cucumber – 1, chopped
- Roma tomatoes – 5, chopped
- Green onions – 5 (both white and green parts), chopped
- Radishes – 5, stems removed, sliced
- Parsley – 2 cups, chopped
- Chopped mint – 1 cup

Lime-vinaigrette
- Juice of 1 ½ lime
- Extra virgin olive oil – 1/3 cup
- Salt and pepper
- Ground sumac – 1 tsp.
- Ground cinnamon – ¼ tsp.
- Ground allspice – ¼ tsp.

Method
1. In a pan, heat 3 tbsp. olive oil.
2. Break the pita bread into pieces and place in the pan.
3. Stir-fry until browned. Add sumac, salt, and pepper.
4. Remove pita chips and drain on paper towels.
5. In a bowl, combine green onions, tomatoes, cucumber, lettuce, radish, and parsley.
6. Whisk together the lime vinaigrette ingredients in a bowl.
7. Dress salad with vinaigrette and toss.
8. Add pita chips and toss to mix.
9. Serve.

Nutritional Facts Per Serving
- Calories: 345
- Fat: 20.4g
- Carb: 39.8g
- Protein: 9.1g

Mediterranean Tuna Salad with Vinaigrette

Prep time: 15 minutes	Total time: 15 minutes	Servings: 6

Ingredients for the vinaigrette
- Dijon mustard – 2 ½ tsp.
- Zest of 1 lime

- Juice of 1 ½ lime
- Extra virgin olive oil – 1/3 cup
- Sumac – ½ tsp.
- Salt and pepper
- Crushed red pepper flakes – ½ tsp.

For the tuna salad
- Genova tuna in olive oil – 3 (5-oz.) cans
- Celery – 2 ½ stalks, chopped
- English cucumber – ½, chopped
- Whole small radishes – 4 to 5, stems removed, chopped
- Green onions – 3, both white and green parts, chopped
- Red onion – ½, chopped
- Pitted Kalamata olives – ½ cup, halved
- Parsley – 1 bunch, chopped
- Mint – 10 to 15, chopped
- Heirloom tomatoes – 6 slices
- Pita chips for serving

Method
1. To make the vinaigrette, whisk together lime zest, lime juice, and mustard in a bowl. Add crushed pepper flakes, salt, pepper, sumac, and olive oil. Whisk to mix. Set aside.

2. To make the salad, combine tuna from cans with mint, parsley, olive, and vegetables. Mix.
3. Drizzle the salad with vinaigrette. Mix, refrigerate for 30 minutes and serve.

Nutritional Facts Per Serving
- Calories: 299
- Fat: 19.2g
- Carb: 6.6g
- Protein: 25.7g

3-Ingredient Mediterranean Salad

Prep time: 10 minutes	Total time: 10 minutes	Servings: 4

Ingredients
- Roma tomatoes – 6, diced
- English cucumber – 1 large, diced
- Chopped parsley – ½ to ¾ cup
- Salt and black pepper to taste
- Ground sumac – 1 tsp.
- Extra virgin olive oil – 2 tbsp.
- Lemon juice – 2 tsp.

Method
1. Add parsley, cucumber, and tomatoes in a bowl.
2. Add salt and set aside for 5 minutes.
3. Add remaining ingredients and mix.
4. Set aside for a few minutes and serve.

Nutritional Facts Per Serving
- Calories: 105
- Fat: 7.5g
- Carb: 9.8g
- Protein: 2.3g

Roasted Asparagus Salad with Tomato and Basil

Prep time: 10 minutes	Cook time: 20 minutes	Servings: 6

Ingredients
- Asparagus – 1.5 lb. trimmed
- Salt
- Extra virgin olive oil – 2 tbsp., and more as needed
- Halloumi cheese – 4 oz. sliced into squares
- Grape tomatoes – 3 cups, halved
- Basil leaves – 15, torn

For the sherry vinaigrette
- White wine vinegar or sherry reserve vinegar – ¼ cup

- Extra virgin olive oil – ¼ cup
- Garlic – 1 clove, minced
- Sumac spice – 1 tsp.
- Salt and pepper

Method

1. Preheat the oven to 400F.
2. Grease a baking dish and place the asparagus spears on it.
3. Sprinkle with salt and drizzle with olive oil. Toss to coat and spread in a single layer.
4. Roast in the oven until tender, about 15 to 20 minutes. Remove from the oven and cool.
5. In a skillet, heat 2 tbsp. olive oil.
6. Place cheese squares, and fry them in batches, about 1 to 2 minutes per side. Remove when golden brown. Drain excess oils and set aside.
7. To make the vinaigrette, whisk together the olive oil with vinegar, salt, pepper, sumac, and garlic.
8. Combine the grape tomatoes with fried cheese in a bowl. Toss to coat with sherry vinaigrette.
9. Assemble the roasted asparagus on a platter.
10. Top with cheese mixture and tomato.
11. Add basil leaves and serve.

Nutritional Facts Per Serving
- Calories: 134
- Fat: 9.5g
- Carb: 10.3g
- Protein: 3.4g

Chapter 15: Pasta and Couscous

Mediterranean Bean and Broccoli Pasta

Prep time: 10 minutes	Cook time: 20 minutes	Servings: 6

Ingredients
- Whole wheat elbow macaroni – ¾ lb.
- Extra virgin olive oil – ¼ cup
- Small red onion – 1, finely chopped
- Garlic – 6 to 8 cloves, minced
- Dried oregano – ½ tsp.
- Aleppo pepper – ½ tsp.
- Crushed red pepper – ¼ tsp.
- Frozen broccoli florets – 1 lb. thawed
- Cannellini beans – 1 can, drained and rinsed
- Salt and pepper
- Chopped fresh parsley – 2 cups
- Mediterranean spice blend – 1 ½ tsp.
- Grated parmesan cheese – 1/3 cup
- Toasted pine nuts – 1/3 cup

Method
1. Cook pasta according to package direction until al dente. Reserve 1 cup of the cooking water and drain the pasta.

2. Heat olive oil in a large pot.
3. Add chopped onions and stir-fry for 2 minutes.
4. Add crushed pepper flakes, Aleppo pepper, oregano, and garlic. Stir-fry until fragrant.
5. Add the broccoli florets and cook for 4 minutes.
6. Add the beans and cook for 3 minutes. Season with salt and pepper.
7. Add pasta and 1/3 cup of the cooking liquid.
8. Add Mediterranean spice blend, Parmesan, and parsley.
9. Toss and adjust seasoning.
10. Sprinkle with toasted pine nuts and serve.

Nutritional Facts Per Serving
- Calories: 367
- Fat: 11.8g
- Carb: 57.8g
- Protein: 13g

Shrimp Avocado Mediterranean Pasta Salad

Prep time: 15 minutes	Cook time: 10 minutes	Servings: 6

Ingredients
- Lemon juice – ¼ cup
- Lemon zest – 1 tsp.

- Dried oregano – 1 tbsp.
- Sweet Spanish paprika – 1 tsp.
- Salt and pepper
- Extra virgin olive oil – 1/3 cup

For pasta salad
- Elbow pasta – 2 cups
- Chopped fresh parsley – 1 cup
- Chopped mint – 1 cup
- Chopped red onions – ½ cup
- Green pepper – 1, chopped
- Cherry tomatoes – 1 pint, halved
- Kalamata olives – ½ cup, chopped
- Pepper flakes to taste
- Avocados – 2 to 3, chopped
- Cooked large shrimp – 12 oz.
- Greek feta cheese – 4 oz. crumbled

Method
1. Cook pasta according to package direction until al dente then drain.
2. Meanwhile, make the dressing: in a bowl, whisk salt, pepper, spices, garlic, lemon juice, and zest. Whisk in olive oil until smooth.
3. Add the pasta to the dressing.

4. Add the remaining ingredients except for feta, shrimp, and avocado. Toss to mix well. Set aside to cool.
5. Add shrimp and avocado before serving. Drizzle with olive oil and toss to combine.
6. Taste and adjust seasoning as desired.
7. Serve.

Nutritional Facts Per Serving
- Calories: 337
- Fat: 18.6g
- Carb: 28.6g
- Protein: 16.6g

Mediterranean Olive Oil Pasta

| Prep time: 10 minutes | Cook time: 9 minutes | Servings: 6 |

Ingredients
- Thin spaghetti – 1 lb.
- Olive oil – ½ cup
- Garlic – 4 cloves, crushed
- Salt
- Chopped fresh parsley – 1 cup
- Grape tomatoes – 12 oz. halved
- Scallions – 3, both green and white part chopped
- Black pepper – 1 tsp.

- Marinated artichoke hearts – 6 oz. drained
- Pitted olives – ¼ cup, halved
- Crumbled feta cheese – ¼ cup
- Fresh basil leaves – 10 to 15, torn
- Zest of 1 lemon
- Crushed red pepper flakes

Method
1. Cook the spaghetti pasta according to package instructions. Drain and return to its cooking pot.
2. Meanwhile, heat the extra virgin olive oil in a skillet.
3. Lower the heat and add garlic and salt. Stir-fry for 10 seconds.
4. Stir in chopped scallions, tomatoes, and parsley. Cover and warm on low heat for 30 seconds.
5. Add warmed olive oil sauce to the pasta and toss to coat.
6. Add black pepper and toss to coat.
7. Add the remaining ingredients and toss to coat well.
8. Serve.

Nutritional Facts Per Serving
- Calories: 389
- Fat: 16.6g
- Carb: 51.1g

- Protein: 10.7g

Mediterranean Pasta

| Prep time: 5 minutes | Cook time: 15 minutes | Servings: 6 |

Ingredients
- Salt – 1 tsp.
- Whole wheat angel hair pasta – 6 ounces
- Garlic – 4 cloves
- Grape tomatoes – 2 cups
- Quartered artichoke hearts – 1 can
- Whole pitted black olives – 1 can
- Olive oil – 3 tbsp.
- Ground black pepper – ½ tsp.
- Crushed red pepper flakes – ¼ tsp.
- Lemon juice – ¼ cup
- Grated parmesan cheese – ¼ cup
- Fresh Italian parsley – ¼ cup

Method
1. Cook pasta according to package direction. Reserve ½ cup of the pasta and then drain.
2. Meanwhile, prepare the vegetables.
3. In a skillet, heat the olive oil over medium heat.

4. Add 1 tsp. salt, pepper, crushed red pepper flakes, garlic, and tomatoes. Stir-fry until garlic is fragrant, about 1 to 2 minutes.
5. Add the pasta to the skillet and toss to coat.
6. Add the olives and artichokes. Drizzle some lemon juice and stir-fry for 1 to 2 minutes.
7. Taste and adjust seasoning. Add a bit of reserved pasta water if the pasta is too dry.
8. Remove from heat and sprinkle with parsley and Parmesan.
9. Toss and serve.

Nutritional Facts Per Serving
- Calories: 267
- Fat: 13g
- Carb: 27g
- Protein: 18g

Quick Mediterranean Pasta

Prep time: 10 minutes	Cook time: 15 minutes	Servings: 4

Ingredients
- Olive oil – 3 tbsp.
- Skinless boneless chicken breasts – 1 pound
- Sun-dried tomatoes – 1 cup, julienned

- Garlic – 2 tbsp. minced
- Fresh angel hair pasta – 1 pound
- Fresh basil – ¼ cup
- Artichoke hearts in water - 1 cup (quartered and drained)
- Kalamata olives – ½ cup, pitted
- Feta cheese – 6 ounces, crumbled
- Heavy cream – ¼ cup
- Dried oregano – 2 tsp.
- Salt and pepper to taste

Method

1. Cook pasta according to package direction until al dente. Drain.
2. Heat olive oil in a skillet over medium heat.
3. Brown chicken strips in the oil, about 3 minutes per side.
4. Then add the garlic and sun dried tomatoes to the skillet and stir-fry for 2 minutes.
5. Now add the feta cheese, olives, basil, and artichoke hearts to the skillet.
6. Transfer the pasta to a bowl and add the chicken sauté to the pasta and toss.
7. Season with salt, pepper, and oregano.
8. Serve.

Nutritional Facts Per Serving
- Calories: 714
- Fat: 29.3g
- Carb: 70.8g
- Protein: 42g

Mediterranean Pearl Couscous

Prep time: 15 minutes	Cook time: 10 minutes	Servings: 6

Ingredients for vinaigrette
- Juice of 1 lemon
- Extra virgin olive oil – 1/3 cup
- Dill weed – 1 tsp.
- Garlic powder – 1 tsp.
- Salt and pepper

For the Couscous
- Pearl couscous – 2 cups
- Extra virgin olive oil
- Water
- Grape tomatoes – 2 cups, halved
- Finely chopped red onions – 1/3 cup
- English cucumber – ½ finely chopped
- Chickpeas – 15 oz. can

- Artichoke hearts – 14 oz. can, chopped
- Pitted Kalamata olives – ½ cup
- Fresh basil – 15 to 20, chopped
- Fresh baby mozzarella – 3 oz.

Method
1. Whisk together the vinaigrette ingredients in a bowl. Set aside.
2. Heat 2 tbsp. olive oil in a pot.
3. Sauté the couscous in the oil until golden brown.
4. Add 3 cups boiling water and cook according to the package. Drain.
5. In a bowl, combine the remaining ingredients except for the mozzarella and basil.
6. Add the basil and couscous then mix.
7. Whisk the vinaigrette and add to the couscous.
8. Mix and adjust seasoning.
9. Mix in the mozzarella and garnish with more basil.
10. Serve.

Nutritional Facts Per Serving
- Calories: 393
- Fat: 13g
- Carb: 57g
- Protein: 13.1g

Mediterranean Couscous Salad

Prep time: 20 minutes	Total time: 1 hour 20 minutes	Servings: 8

Ingredients
- Chicken broth – 1 cup
- Uncooked couscous – ¾ cup
- Cubed Roma tomatoes – 1 cup
- Cubed unpeeled cucumber – 1 cup
- Halved pitted Kalamata olives – ½ cup
- Chopped green onions – ¼ cup
- Chopped fresh dill weed – ¼ cup
- Lemon juice – 2 tbsp.
- Olive oil – 2 tbsp.
- Salt – 1/8 tsp.
- Crumbled feta cheese – 2 tbsp.

Method
1. Heat broth to boiling, and add the couscous. Remove from the heat and let stand for 5 minutes, covered.
2. In a bowl, place onions, dill weed, olives, cucumber, and tomatoes. Stir in the couscous.
3. Beat oil, salt, and lemon juice until well blended.
4. Pour over vegetable mixture and mix.
5. Cover and keep in the refrigerator for 1 hour.
6. Sprinkle with cheese and serve.

Nutritional Facts Per Serving
- Calories: 120
- Fat: 5g
- Carb: 16g
- Protein: 3g

Crunchy Mediterranean Couscous Salad

| Prep time: 15 minutes | Cook time: 5 minutes | Servings: 6 |

Ingredients
- Cooked couscous – 2 cups
- Chopped broccoli florets – 1 cup
- English cucumber – 1, seeded and chopped
- Red bell pepper – 1, seeded and chopped
- Fresh tomato – 1 chopped
- Chickpeas – 1 (15-ounce) can, drained and rinsed
- Crumbled feta cheese – ½ cup
- Homemade lemon vinaigrette

Method
1. Prepare couscous and cool to room temperature.
2. Toss chopped veggies, couscous, and feta.
3. Season with salt and pepper.
4. Toss in the dressing, a few tbsp. at a time.
5. Serve.

Nutritional Facts Per Serving
- Calories: 232
- Fat: 3g
- Carb: 50g
- Protein: 10g

Mediterranean Couscous Salad II

| Prep time: 20 minutes | Cook time: 10 minutes | Servings: 6 |

Ingredients for the dressing
- Lemon juice – 4 tbsp.
- White wine vinegar – 1 tbsp.
- Olive oil – 2 tbsp.
- Garlic – 2 cloves, minced
- Sugar -1 tsp.
- Italian seasoning – 1 tbsp.
- Salt to taste
- Pepper to taste

Salad
- Couscous – ¾ cup, uncooked
- Butter – 1 tbsp.
- English cucumber – 1, chopped
- Cherry tomatoes – 1 cup, halved

- Olives – ½ cup, sliced
- Green pepper – 1, chopped
- Medium red onion – 1/2, chopped
- Feta cheese – ¾ cup, crumbled
- Mint – 3 tbsp. chopped

Method
1. Cook the couscous according to package instructions. Then add the butter and cool.
2. Whisk all the dressing ingredients in a bowl.
3. Add the couscous to a large bowl and fluff with a fork.
4. Add the rest of the salad ingredients.
5. Pour the prepared dressing over and toss to mix.
6. Serve.

Nutritional Facts Per Serving
- Calories: 231
- Fat: 12g
- Carb: 24g
- Protein: 6g

Mediterranean Couscous Salad III

Prep time: 20 minutes	Cook time: 10 minutes	Servings: 6

Ingredients for couscous

- Water – 1 cup
- Instant couscous – 6 ounces
- Kosher salt – ½ tsp.
- Extra-virgin olive oil – 2 tbsp.

Salad
- Diced Roma tomatoes – ½ cup
- Diced English cucumber – ½ cup
- Diced red bell pepper – ½ cup
- Canned garbanzo beans – ½ cup
- Minced red onion – ¼ cup
- Kalamata olives – ½ cup, pitted and sliced
- Feta cheese – 2 tbsp.
- Chopped parsley – 1 tsp.
- Chopped mint – 1 tsp.
- Chopped basil – 1 tsp.
- Dried oregano – ¼ tsp.

Lemon dressing
- Lemon zest – 1 tsp.
- Lemon juice – 2 tbsp.
- Red wine vinegar – 1 tbsp.
- Salt – ¼ tsp.
- Black pepper – ¼ tsp.

Method
1. In a pan, add the water, salt, and olive oil. Bring to a boil, add couscous and stir quickly. Turn off the heat and cover.
2. Let couscous stand for 5 minutes, then fluff with a fork and cool.
3. Salad: combine red onion, beans, bell pepper, cucumber, tomatoes, couscous, olives, oregano, basil, mint, parsley, and cheese in a bowl.
4. Whisk the dressing ingredients in a bowl.
5. Pour dressing over the salad. Stir to combine.
6. Serve.

Nutritional Facts Per Serving
- Calories: 91
- Fat: 7g
- Carb: 3g
- Protein: 1g

Company Couscous

| Prep time: 5 minutes | Cook time: 35 minutes | Servings: 4 |

Ingredients
- Couscous – 1 cup

- Boiling water – 1 cup
- Olive oil – 3 tbsp.
- Garlic – 1 clove, minced
- Diced red bell pepper – ¼ cup
- Green onions – 4, sliced
- Cherry tomatoes – 1 cup
- Fresh basil leaves – 1 cup
- Salt
- Ground black pepper
- Balsamic vinegar – 1 dash
- Grated Parmesan cheese – ¼ cup

Method

1. Preheat the oven to 350F.
2. Add couscous into boiling water and bring to a boil.
3. Cover and remove from heat. Let stand for 5 minutes, then fluff with a fork.
4. Meanwhile, in a skillet, heat oil over medium heat.
5. Stir in peppers, green onions, and garlic. Sauté briefly.
6. Then add cooked couscous, basil, tomatoes, salt, and pepper.
7. Mix and transfer to a 1 ½-quart casserole dish. Add vinegar on top.
8. Bake in a preheated 350F oven for 20 minutes.
9. Sprinkle with Parmesan and serve.

Nutritional Facts Per Serving
- Calories: 299
- Fat: 12.4g
- Carb: 38g
- Protein: 9.1g

Chapter 16: Dessert Recipes

No Bake Dessert Bars

| Prep time: 15 minutes | Cook time: 5 minutes | Servings:8 |

Ingredients
- Large Medjool dates – 26, pitted
- Walnut halves – 26
- Unsalted butter – 2 sticks
- Honey – 3 to 4 tbsp.
- Coconut extract – 1 ½ tsp.
- All-purpose flour – 1 ½ cup
- Finely chopped pistachios – 1 cup

Method
1. Stuff each date with a walnut half. Close to enclose the halves.
2. Grease a container and assemble the stuffed dates on it in a single layer.
3. Melt the butter and honey on a pan.
4. Add the coconut extract and flour. Stir for 5 minutes or until golden brown.
5. Pour the flour-honey mixture on top of the dates. Allow to set and top with chopped pistachios.
6. Cut the date cake into bars.
7. Refrigerate for 1 hour and serve.

Nutritional Facts Per Serving
- o   Calories: 509
- o   Fat: 34.2g
- o   Carb: 48.7g
- o   Protein: 7.7g

Greek Honey Cake

| Prep time: 10 minutes | Cook time: 30 minutes | Servings: 15 |

Ingredients for the cake
- o   Eggs – 5
- o   Low-fat Greek yogurt – 1 cup
- o   Granulated sugar – 2 cups
- o   Ground almonds – 5 tbsp.
- o   Zest of 1 lemon
- o   Zest of 1 orange
- o   All-purpose flour – 1 ¼ cup
- o   Coarse semolina – 1 cup
- o   Baking powder – 2 tsp.
- o   Extra virgin olive oil – ¾ cup, plus 1 tbsp.
- o   Shaved almonds for topping – 1 handful

For honey pistachio syrup
- o   Shelled salted pistachios – 1 ¼ cup
- o   Honey – 1 ¼ cup

- Juice of 2 oranges
- Juice of 1 lemon

Method
1. Preheat the oven to 350F.
2. Grease a baking pan (9" x 13") with butter and dust with flour.
3. In a bowl, place all the cake ingredients. Whisk to combine.
4. Pour the batter into the prepared baking pan and spread evenly.
5. Bake until golden, about 25 to 30 minutes. Remove and cool.
6. To prepare the honey syrup: toast the pistachio in a pan.
7. Stir in honey once the pistachios start to smell. Add the lemon and orange juice.
8. Bring to a boil until syrupy, about 1 to 2 minutes.
9. Create holes on the cake with a skewer.
10. Pour the syrup on the cake and spread evenly then sprinkle with almonds.
11. Cut into squares and serve.

Nutritional Facts Per Serving
- Calories: 378
- Fat: 10.3g

- Carb: 66.7g
- Protein: 8g

Honey Bun Cinnamon Cookies

Prep time: 15 minutes	Cook time: 12 minutes	Servings: 48 cookies

Ingredients for the cookie dough

- Powdered sugar – 1 ½ cups, sifted
- Unsalted butter – 1 cup, room temperature
- Salt – ½ tsp.
- Baking powder – ½ tsp.
- Vanilla extract – 2 tsp.
- Egg – 1
- All-purpose flour – 2 ½ cups

Cinnamon filling

- Unsalted butter – 6 tbsp.
- Packed dark brown sugar – ¼ cup
- All-purpose flour – 3 tbsp.
- Honey – 1 tbsp.
- Ground cinnamon – 1 tbsp.
- Ground nutmeg – ½ tsp.

Glaze
- Honey – 2 tbsp.
- Whole milk – 1 tbsp.
- Vanilla extract – 1 tsp.
- Powdered sugar – ½ to ¾ cup, sifted

Other
- Ground cinnamon for dusting

Method
1. To make the cookie dough, in a bowl, combine butter, sugar, salt, and baking powder.
2. Use a hand mixer on low speed to mix and gradually increase speed until creamy.
3. Add the vanilla and beat to mix, then add the egg and beat.
4. Add the flour and mix until dough forms.
5. Shape the dough into a ball. Flatten into a circle then roll into a rectangle (13 x 14-inch).
6. To make the filling: combine the flour, butter, brown sugar, cinnamon, honey, and nutmeg in a bowl. Beat for 2 minutes or until fluffy and light.
7. Spread the filling on the dough to cover the entire surface.
8. Tightly roll up the dough. Wrap the dough with plastic wrap and freeze for 1 hour.

9. Preheat the oven to 350F and line a baking sheet with parchment paper.
10. Remove the dough and remove the wrap.
11. Cut into ¼-inch thick cookie disks and place on the baking sheets.
12. Bake for 12 to 14 minutes, or until cookies turn golden brown. Remove and cool.
13. To make the glaze, combine the glaze ingredients in a bowl and mix.
14. Brush the glaze onto the cooled cookies and dust with cinnamon.
15. Serve.

Nutritional Facts Per Serving
- Calories: 122
- Fat: 5g
- Carb: 19.2g
- Protein: 0.9g

Basbousa

| Prep time: 15 minutes | Cook time: 45 minutes | Servings: 8 |

Ingredients
- Unsalted butter – ½ cup, plus 2 tbsp.

- Sugar – 1 cup
- Plain yogurt – 1 cup
- Fine semolina – 1 cup
- Coarse semolina – 1 cup
- Milk – 1/3 cup
- Baking powder – 1 tsp.
- Sweetened shredded coconut – ¼ cup
- Shaved almonds – ¼ cup

Syrup
- Sugar – 1 ½ cup
- Water – 1 ¾ cup
- Short cinnamon stick - 1
- Lemon juice – ¼ tsp.

Method
1. Preheat the oven to 350F.
2. Melt the butter in the microwave and set aside.
3. Combine yogurt and sugar in a bowl. Add the milk, baking powder and semolina.
4. Stir in melted butter and set aside for a few minutes.
5. Lightly grease a 9-inch round cake pan and pour in the semolina mixture.
6. Bake in the oven for 40 to 45 minutes at 350F. Broil briefly if you want color.

7. Meanwhile, make the syrup: in a pot, combine water, sugar, and cinnamon.
8. Bring to a boil, then lower the heat to simmer. Continue to stir until syrup thickens.
9. Remove from the heat and stir in the lemon juice. Cool and remove the cinnamon.
10. Remove the basbousa from the oven and instantly pour the cool syrup on the hot basbousa.
11. Cool completely. Top with coconut and almonds.
12. Slice and serve.

Nutritional Facts Per Serving
- Calories: 625
- Fat: 22g
- Carb: 99.8g
- Protein: 9.7g

French Pear Tart

| Prep time: 15 minutes | Cook time: 1 minute | Servings: 8 |

Ingredients for the crust
- All-purpose flour – 1 ½ cups
- Sugar – 5 tbsp.
- Salt – ½ tsp.
- Unsalted butter – 12 tbsp. melted

Filling

- Large pears – 8, washed and sliced into ½ inch slices
- Unsalted butter – 3 tbsp.
- Water – 1 tbsp.
- Fig preserves – ¾ cup
- Salt – ¼ tsp.

Method

1. Place one rack to the middle and one on top. Preheat the oven to 350F.
2. In a bowl, mix sugar, flour, and salt. Add melted butter and mix to make a dough.
3. Transfer dough to a 9-inch tart pan. Use your hands to spread the dough on the bottom and onto the rims of the pan.
4. Bake on the middle rack until crust turns golden brown, about 30 minutes.
5. Remove and let cool. Keep the oven on.
6. Heat the fig preserves in the microwave for 40 seconds and strain.
7. In a skillet, heat 1 tbsp. butter. Add 1 tbsp. water and 5 sliced pears.
8. Cook for 3 minutes, or until slightly tender. Remove and cool.

9. Melt 2 tbsp. butter in the same skillet and add the remaining 3 sliced pears, salt, and chunks of fig preserves.
10. Cover and cook on medium heat until very tender, about 10 minutes.
11. Mash the cooked pears mixture into a puree with a potato masher.
12. Cook until pureed mixture thickens, about 5 to 7 minutes.
13. Spread the pear-fig puree evenly onto the cooled crust.
14. Arrange the cooled pear slices in layered circles on top.
15. Place the tart on the middle rack of the oven and bake for 30 minutes at 350F.
16. Then remove the tart from the oven and brush surface with warmed fig liquid.
17. Return to the oven and place on the top rack.
18. Broil until tart gets a caramelized look. Watch carefully.
19. Remove from the oven and cool for 1 ½ hours before serving.
20. Slice and serve.

Nutritional Facts Per Serving
- Calories: 448
- Fat: 22.1g

- Carb: 63g
- Protein: 3.5g

Baklava

Prep time: 25 minutes	Cook time: 45 minutes	Servings: 36

Ingredients
- Shelled pistachios – 6 oz. chopped (set aside 3 to 4 tbsp. for garnish)
- Walnuts – 6 oz. chopped
- Hazelnuts – 6 oz. chopped
- Sugar – ¼ cup
- Ground cinnamon – 2 tbsp.
- Ground cloves – 1 large pinch
- Phyllo dough – 16 oz. thawed
- Unsalted butter – 18 tbsp. melted

Honey syrup
- Sugar – ¾ cup
- Cold water – 1 cup
- Honey – 1 cup
- Orange extract – 1 tbsp.
- Whole cloves – 5
- Juice of 1 lemon

Method

1. In a bowl, combine pistachios, ground cloves, cinnamon, and ¼-cup sugar. Stir to mix.
2. Preheat the oven to 350F.
3. Grease a baking dish with melted butter. Place one phyllo sheet on the baking sheet. Brush with butter and fold in any excess.
4. Repeat with phyllo sheets and butter until you have used up 1/3 of the phyllo package. Spread half of the nut mixture evenly over the top sheet.
5. Layer another 1/3 of the phyllo sheets on top (brush each with butter) and spread the remaining half of the nut mixture on the top layer.
6. Layer the remaining phyllo sheets. Trim any excess phyllo and brush the top layer with more butter.
7. Cut ½-inch deep, diagonal lines in the phyllo and make 1 ½-inch diamond pieces. Don't cut all the way down.
8. Bake on a low rack until golden, about 45 minutes to 1 hour. Insert a skewer and check. Check the baklava halfway through baking.
9. Meanwhile, make the honey syrup: add sugar and water in a saucepan. Heat and stir occasionally until sugar dissolves.
10. Add the whole cloves, honey, and orange extract.

11. Bring to a boil, lower heat and simmer for 25 minutes. Remove and cool.
12. Remove the whole cloves and add lemon juice.
13. Remove the baklava from the oven and pour the cooled syrup on top.
14. Set aside so the syrup is absorbed.
15. Cut the baklava a few hours later.

Nutritional Facts Per Serving
- Calories: 229
- Fat: 14.5g
- Carb: 23.7g
- Protein: 3.4g

Roasted Peaches and Greek Yogurt Crostini

Prep time: 10 minutes	Cook time: 20 minutes	Servings: 8

Ingredients
- Greek yogurt – 1/3 cup
- Cream cheese – 6 oz. softened
- Zest of one orange
- Sugar – 1/3 cup
- Ground nutmeg – 1 pinch
- Ground cinnamon – 1 pinch

- Peaches – 3, cored and sliced into thin wedges
- Orange juice – 3 tbsp.
- Crostini/French baguette slices – 8, toasted
- Roughly chopped pecan halves – ¼ cup
- Honey to drizzle

Method

1. Blend the sugar, orange zest, cream cheese, yogurt, nutmeg, and cinnamon in a food processor. Blend until fluffy.
2. Place in a bowl and refrigerate until ready to use.
3. Preheat the oven to 425F.
4. In a bowl, mix the orange juice and peaches.
5. Lightly pat dry the peaches. Line a baking sheet with parchment and place the peaches.
6. Bake in the oven for 20 to 25 minutes at 425F.
7. Spread the baguette slices with yogurt mixture and top with chopped pecans and two slices of the roasted peaches.
8. Drizzle a little honey over each crostini and serve.

Nutritional Facts Per Serving

- Calories: 429
- Fat: 27.1g
- Carb: 41.5g

- Protein: 9.6g

Orange Ricotta Cake

| Prep time: 15 minutes | Cook time: 45 minutes | Servings: 12 |

Ingredients
- Butter for the pan
- Brown sugar – ½ cup
- Water – 1 tbsp.
- Zest of 2 oranges, 1 sliced
- Part-skim ricotta – 1 ½ cup
- Extra virgin olive oil – ¼ cup, plus 2 tbsp.
- Vanilla extract – ½ tsp.
- Eggs – 3
- All-purpose flour – 1 ½ cup
- Baking powder – 2 tsp.
- Salt – ¾ tsp.
- Granulated sugar – ¾ cup
- Confectioners' sugar for dusting

Method
1. Preheat the oven to 325F.

2. Grease a 9-inch baking pan with butter (bottom, and the sides) then line the bottom with a parchment paper.
3. Melt the brown sugar in the water to make a thick, pasty slurry. Spread the bottom of the baking pan with the mixture.
4. Arrange the orange slices on the bottom of the pan (on top of the sugar coating).
5. Whisk the olive oil, ricotta, and vanilla in a bowl. One at a time, add the eggs and whisk to mix.
6. Sift flour, salt, and baking powder directly over the wet ingredients. Whisk to mix.
7. Combine the orange zest and sugar then add to the mixture. Mix the batter again to combine well.
8. Pour the batter into the prepared pan and bake in the oven until a toothpick comes out clean (when inserted in the middle), about 45 minutes. Check the cake at 40 minutes mark. The cake can take up to 1 hour. Time depends on the oven.
9. Cool, slice and serve.

Nutritional Facts Per Serving
- Calories: 179
- Fat: 8.4g
- Carb: 20.1g
- Protein: 6.2g

Carrot Cake

Prep time: 10 minutes	Cook time: 1 hour	Servings: 12

Ingredients
- Extra virgin olive oil
- Reduced fat Greek yogurt – ½ cup
- 2% reduced fat milk – 1/3 cup
- Dark honey – ½ cup
- Eggs – 3
- Whole wheat flour – 2 ¼ cup
- Baking powder – 1 ½ tsp.
- Salt – ½ tsp.
- Ground cinnamon – 4 tsp.
- Ground cardamom – ½ tsp.
- Ground ginger – ¼ tsp.
- Finely grated carrots – 2 cups
- Medjool dates – 6, pitted and finely chopped
- Chopped walnuts – 1/3 cup
- Powdered sugar for dusting

Method
1. Preheat the oven to 350F.
2. Whisk milk, yogurt, and olive oil in a bowl. One at a time, add the eggs and whisk to combine.
3. Whisk spices, flour, baking powder, and salt in another bowl.

4. Slowly add the dry ingredients to the wet ingredients. Mix.
5. Fold in carrots, and mix to combine. Then add walnuts and dates. Mix.
6. Line a 9-inch square baking pan with parchment paper and pour the batter into the pan.
7. Bake in the oven for 1 hour at 350F. Check with a toothpick.
8. Cool completely and sprinkle with powdered sugar.
9. Cut into square and serve.

Nutritional Facts Per Serving
- Calories: 167
- Fat: 8.6g
- Carb: 20.2g
- Protein: 5g

Conclusion

The Mediterranean diet offers a host of health benefits, including heart and brain health, weight loss, diabetes control, and cancer prevention. Getting started on a new diet can seem overwhelming. This book will guide you through everything you need to know about the Mediterranean diet. This delectable Mediterranean cookbook gives you over 60 simple and filling meals packed with fresh vegetables, fish, seafood, fruit, whole grains, and heart-healthy olive oil, and will really change your whole life overwhelmingly.

Thank you

Before you go, I just wanted to say thank you for purchasing my book.

You could have picked from dozens of other books on the same topic but you took a chance and chose this one.

So, a HUGE thanks to you for getting this book and for reading all the way to the end.

Now I wanted to ask you for a small favor. **Could you please consider posting a review on the platform? Reviews are one of the easiest ways to support the work of authors.**

This feedback will help me continue to write the type of books that will help you get the results you want. So if you enjoyed it, please let me know.

www.ingramcontent.com/pod-product-compliance
Lightning Source LLC
Chambersburg PA
CBHW052057110526
44591CB00013B/2254